T0274049

COLD★WAR
VIRGINIA

COLD★WAR VIRGINIA

FRANCIS GARY POWERS JR.
AND CHRISTOPHER STURDEVANT

THE
History
PRESS

Published by The History Press
Charleston, SC
www.historypress.com

Copyright © 2024 by Francis Gary Powers Jr. and Christopher Sturdevant
All rights reserved

First published 2024

Manufactured in the United States

ISBN 9781467156653

Library of Congress Control Number: 2024930894

Notice: The information in this book is true and complete to the best of our knowledge. It is offered without guarantee on the part of the authors or The History Press. The authors and The History Press disclaim all liability in connection with the use of this book.

All rights reserved. No part of this book may be reproduced or transmitted in any form whatsoever without prior written permission from the publisher except in the case of brief quotations embodied in critical articles and reviews.

CONTENTS

Introduction to the Cold War   7

1. Project Nike in Virginia: Defending Cold War Skies   19
2. The Cold War and the Race to Space   27
3. The National Reconnaissance Office and Evolution
    of Satellites   41
4. Virginia Military Bases During the Cold War   45
5. Woodrow Wilson and the Origins of the Cold War   67
6. Atoms for Peace: Atomic Energy for Mankind   73
7. Creation of the Central Intelligence Agency   83
8. The Federal Bureau of Investigation:
    Fighting Enemies Within   99
9. Infamous Soviet Moles Arrested by the FBI   109
10. General George C. Marshall and the Marshall Plan   121
11. Francis Gary Powers and the U-2 Incident   129
12. Notable Cold War Virginians   147
13. Doomsday Planning for the Third World War   151

Notes   161
Index   173
About the Authors   176

INTRODUCTION TO THE COLD WAR

WHAT WAS THE COLD WAR?

Where is the "Old War Museum"? Where is the "Cold Water Museum"? During our decades of promoting Cold War history—whether it be lecturing, presenting or writing on the era—we have received these and other puzzling questions when discussing the longest and costliest conflict in American history. These questions, oftentimes accompanied by blank stares, have affirmed the need to educate a generation born after the 1980s.

In the United States, many who grew up and were alive during the Cold War were largely not directly affected. This is primarily due to the Cold War being fought elsewhere, projecting American power away from the homeland in places such as Berlin, Southeast Asia, Nicaragua and other far-flung places around the globe. Attempting to explain this frightening era that sought to prevent a Third World War, and the fight against the Communist march of the twentieth century, has been a challenging but laudable undertaking.

Depending on the era, we watched news stories unfold on television sets about the Chernobyl disaster and the space shuttle *Challenger* explosion, JFK's assassination and the Apollo 11 moon landing. We read newspaper accounts of the Solidarity movement in Poland or, as children, read *Weekly Reader* accounts about how cockroaches would be the only species able to survive an otherwise certain nuclear war.

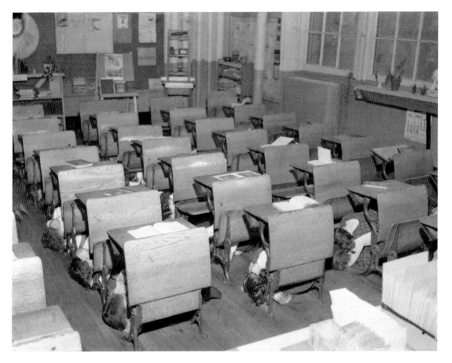

Duck and Cover drills were common for children growing up during the Cold War era. *Wikimedia Commons.*

But the full story of the Cold War is slowly coming into focus. Over thirty years after the fall of the Berlin Wall, information is gradually being made available from many sources as to just how close a Third World War came. To aid this understanding, heretofore classified information has been declassified and disseminated through different information channels over the years, shedding light on many facets of activity from all sides of the conflict. More frightening nuclear weapons were errantly dropped on or near civilian areas, with the exact whereabouts of many remaining unknown. Soviet military officers thankfully overrode the urge to retaliate with nuclear weapons because of faulty data over their computer systems that showed American launches toward the Union of Soviet Socialist Republics (USSR). Nike missile accidents resulted in an explosion on a base in New Jersey in 1958. These and other stories of the Cold War have caused great consternation.

A BRIEF INTRODUCTION TO THE COLD WAR

With the Second World War drawn to a close, and the National Socialists in Nazi Germany relegated to the ash bin of history, the world was made safe for two remaining superpowers. The dawn of the Cold War would see the United States and the Soviet Union (Russia) standing toe to toe on land, sea and air across the globe for forty-six years. Since the first atomic bomb was tested and used to end the Second World War in 1945, both superpowers raced to yield more destructive weapons to outdo each other. Hence, what would ensue was the threat of nuclear war that would be a fear for decades in the postwar era. Along with their allies, both the United States and the Soviet Union set out to dominate the land, air, sea and space, as those mediums would become the focus of outmaneuvering the other side.

Europe had been destroyed, weakened by years of war, and alliances were sought to form stronger positions in Europe, both from the U.S.-led and Soviet-controlled countries. On behalf of the West, the North Atlantic Treaty Organization (NATO) was formed in 1949, aligning together in case of the very real possibility of Soviet attack. As American troops were recalled from Europe, the Soviet troops never left. Stalin used the vague terms of elections and postwar peace agreements to have Communism take hold of other Eastern and Central European governments, such as Poland and Czechoslovakia and others. These countries aligned by forming the Warsaw Pact in 1955.

BERLIN

A conflict over Berlin broke out almost immediately when the Soviets blockaded that city in 1948. Like Germany itself, the city of Berlin had also been divided between East and West Berlin, with Soviet control over East Berlin and Allied control over West Berlin. Deep inside what officially became East Germany in 1949, Berlin was considered a land-island surrounded by hostility. Soviet leader Joseph Stalin was determined to choke the city off from the Allies and force the Western powers out of Berlin. Through the treaty at the Potsdam conference in 1945, the West had access to the Allied Berlin sector through roads and air corridors. President Truman, in a show of resolve, stood with the citizens of West Berlin. Instead of direct confrontation, the Berlin Airlift was created.

Lieutenant Colonel James R. Dawley Sr., Berlin Air Safety Center, Germany, 1948/49. BASC was one of only two shared commands with the USSR during the Cold War. *Courtesy of MJ Dawley.*

For nearly a year, the West Berliners were supplied with fuel, coal, medicines, foodstuffs and other supplies. The crisis was averted. A pilot named Colonel Gail Halvorsen became known as the Candy Bomber and Uncle Wiggly Wings. He and other pilots flying into West Berlin parachuted candy, chocolate and gum to the children of Berlin as they stood near the drop sites. Through action, the United States would not abandon West Berlin and its citizens. The Soviets finally backed down and restored access

USAF Colonel Gail
Halverson during the
Berlin Airlift. *Joint Base
San Antonio photograph.*

Lieutenant Colonel James R. Dawley Sr., Tegel Air Tower Berlin, Germany, 1948/49.
During his thirty-two-year career, Dawley also served at Langley AFB, assigned to RB-66
and later EB-111 electronic warfare programs. *Courtesy of MJ Dawley.*

to the city of West Berlin. The Cold War was well underway, and this event drew the battle lines of this new world reality.

In the 1950s, higher-yield nuclear bombs were researched and developed, and production increased exponentially by both sides. War broke out in 1950 on the Korean peninsula, a short time after China fell to Mao Tse Tung and the Communists. The Soviets raced ahead into space with the Sputnik satellite in 1957, and Cuba became a focal point in 1959 with the rise of Fidel Castro. As the Soviets gained an ally off the shores of Florida, Cuba became the stage of a missile crisis in 1962, nearly bringing the world to the brink of nuclear war. The war in Vietnam took hold well into the 1970s, and with the election of Ronald Reagan, a new attitude of peace through strength was a diversion from detents and perceived weakness abroad from the lingering effects of failed domestic policies, Vietnam syndrome and the Iran hostage crisis of 1979.

Contrary to widespread belief, the Cold War was anything but "peaceful." The Cold War was truly dangerous and deadly, fraught with conflicts from Asia to Africa, Korea and Vietnam to Angola. Nuclear war was the penultimate outcome, a certain Armageddon that could destroy humanity. The Cold War was truly a world war, fought and challenged across the

Arlington National Cemetery, Major Willard George Palm. RB-47H mission shot down by Soviet Defense forces over the Barents Sea, July 1, 1960. *Library of Congress.*

globe. Training accidents were more common than the public was led to believe. Men were lost on submarines such as USS *Cochino*, USS *Thresher* and USS *Scorpion*. Due to ever-increasing needs for information on the other side, the United States sent many dangerous reconnaissance missions behind the Iron Curtain. American planes were shot down over Eastern Europe. U.S. military personnel are still listed as missing in action from missions setting out to assess the response of Warsaw Pact and Soviet radar systems.

COLLAPSE OF THE SOVIET UNION

In the 1980s, with the ascension of President Ronald Reagan in the United States and Mikhail Gorbachev in the Soviet Union, a new era of discussion ensued, ranging from nuclear weapons reductions and opening of the Soviet society to greater self-expression. President Reagan rebuilt the U.S. military, fostered a harsher tone toward the existence of an "Evil Empire" and sought technological advantage researching SDI (Strategic Defense Initiative) to shoot down incoming Soviet missiles, launched either accidentally or by design.

President Ronald Reagan at the Berlin Wall in 1987. *Reagan White House Photographs.*

Chernobyl Reactor #4 in 1986, Ukraine, USSR. *IAEA Image Bank.*

Reagan and Gorbachev sign the Intermediate Nuclear Forces reduction (INF) agreement. *Reagan White House Photographs.*

The Chernobyl disaster in 1986, mounting losses inside Afghanistan and a stagnant economy in the Soviet Union, coupled with military pressure from the United States and its allies, hastened the collapse of the Soviet Union. In 1989, the Berlin Wall fell. Unlike decades prior, when the Soviet Union rolled into breakaway Warsaw Pact countries with tanks and infantry, the Soviets withheld the use of force. As countries under the thumb of the Soviets declared their independence, the Soviet Union finally officially collapsed in 1991. It marked the disastrous end of the Communist experiment in Russia.

WHAT HAPPENED TO THE COLD WAR?

Of course, the context of the Cold War is long gone, having been left to books about various historical events of the twentieth century and artifact relics in museums. The Cold War era seemed to simply disappear after the fall of the Berlin Wall in 1989. Two years later, the Cold War whimpered to a close with the subsequent dissolution of the Soviet Union in 1991. No ticker tape parades took place. No large-scale celebrations were held in the streets. No Nuremberg Trials similar to those after the Second World War were convened for war crimes by the defunct Soviet Union and its Warsaw Pact alliance. Time simply kept marching along as if the Cold War never really occurred here in the United States.

It was an era when record players and rotary phones were high-tech, James Bond worked covertly to stop the villains and being a superhero actually meant something—like Superman's peace, justice and the American way. The lexicon and symbols of the Cold War have, not surprisingly, changed as well. There is no Berlin Wall surrounding that city, and no longer does an "iron curtain" dominate the landscape across Eastern and Central Europe. Also absent are the high-level summits that took place, with the chattering class in Washington, D.C., talking up a peaceful approach to solving the Cold War. Nike today is known as a shoe company. Few would confuse Nike with nuclear-equipped missile systems deployed around the United States to shoot down long-range Soviet bombers. Not to be forgotten, U2 is a famous rock band, not a spy plane— and a Bay of Pigs sounds downright cruel.

Humor aside, the Cold War's importance should not be underestimated, as it overshadowed and shaped our entire American way of life in the twentieth century and beyond. Militaries were sustained, diplomacy undertaken, foreign aid given to rebuild and sustain countries, weapons systems developed and even a national highway system was built in the United States. Preservation efforts and attention to this fascinating era are underserved, and proper recognition of the tens of millions of Cold War veterans has been lacking. Authoring this book on the Cold War in the Commonwealth of Virginia is the latest in the series of The History Press, continuing the fascination of the important local stories of the Cold War.

WHAT THIS BOOK IS ABOUT

The Commonwealth of Virginia is unique in its proximity to the power brokers of Washington, D.C. It was smack-dab in the middle of decision-making, war production, deployments, direction by leaders. Geographically speaking, the United States was far away from the events unfolding around the rest of the world after the Second World War. Short of serving in the armed forces; those with relatives in war zones especially hit such as Europe, Asia or Latin America; or spending extended time abroad, many Americans were not directly affected by the Soviet Union and its reach. Thus, as Americans, too often we thought of the Cold War as ephemeral or occurring somewhere else: Berlin, Cuba, Vietnam, Korea and so on. But where did the men and women who served in the armed forces come from? Where did Cold War munitions, trucks, ships and other war support initiate? How about our politicians, diplomats and others who would figure so prominently in many Cold War events?

After all, a young man named Francis Gary Powers from a farm in rural Pound, Virginia, became an unexpected focal point and symbol of the Cold War. To defend the skies of the Commonwealth from the threat of Soviet long-range bombers, eleven Nike missile systems were deployed around the Norfolk and Washington, D.C. metropolitan areas. After years of uncoordinated intelligence operations throughout the federal government, intelligence operations became centralized with headquarters in Langley, Virginia, after the Second World War. The Radford Ammunition plant produced propellants in the mountains of southwest Virginia to aid war production against Communist-backed adversaries, primarily in Korea and Vietnam. As the Space Race evolved in the 1950s, NASA Langley was created as a governing body. Cold War military bases of all branches of the United States continue to have a large presence today. Tying together these and other sites of importance, events and personalities of the Cold War era is a challenging task, one that is akin to a jigsaw puzzle that can be used to educate this fascinating era of history unlike any other.

This book is meant to be an educational undertaking of Cold War heritage and an erstwhile look at the role of Virginia within the context of the larger struggle between the United States and the Soviet Union. It is not meant to be an exhaustive, definitive work, since entire volumes have previously and continue to be examined and written on a plethora of aspects of the Cold War. In all, we hope to share with the reader how the Cold War legacy has had a lasting impact on the Commonwealth of Virginia and around the world. In the end, we sincerely hope you, as the reader, will find this work enjoyable and interesting, perhaps even recalling this fascinating history for those who lived through the latter part of the twentieth century.

1

PROJECT NIKE IN VIRGINIA

DEFENDING COLD WAR SKIES

A bout 265 Nike missile sites were established in the United States to become the next generation of anti-aircraft weapons to deter invasion by an enemy air force after the Second World War. The Nike missiles were a last line of defense for those long-range Soviet bombers. The missile sites operated under NORAD control (North American Air Defense Command). The overall defense plan was to engage Soviet incursions into Canada and off the coastlines where the population was more sparsely located to minimize casualties. The Distant Early Warning Line (DEW Line), Near Canada Line, then followed by the Nike Missile sites, would take their place as the last-ditch attempt to take out any remaining bombers. According to many Nike missile veterans over the years, they noted there was nowhere to hide from nuclear fallout should Hercules missiles be deployed over these civilian areas. Radiation would affect the total environment, including the air, water and food supplies. In any event, the missileers would be lucky to fire off one or two missiles at this stage of an invasion. If the bombers reached this far, they concluded, devastation was the only recourse for all involved.

The Nike missile systems were established around major metropolitan areas all over the United States, including Virginia and the Washington, D.C. area. They were often in a multi-city configuration that fell under a command structure HQ, and various radar systems in different areas would communicate with each other. Nike bases were active-duty U.S. Army sites where young men were assigned from such technical training bases as Fort Ord in California. These young men worked, lived and trained as they grew into manhood. It was common for men to marry local women, start families and continue to live in the community near the bases at which they were stationed. When the Nike Hercules was more fully integrated and the Vietnam War started to escalate, the Army scaled back the number of bases in the United States. Many of these bases were taken over by various state National Guard commands, as the Army was allocating more funding to the Vietnam War.

The Nike sites in each city underwent a familiar design. Two parcels of land in each city, noted for their highest points in that locale, were selected for locations of fire control and launch areas. The highest points were selected so as to not interfere with radar tracking. The fire control area served not only as a base for the radar towers but also housing. The typical base had a barracks, mess hall, officers' club, chapel and recreation facilities. Some also had a basketball court and hobby shop. The launch area was approximately two miles away as the crow flies, where the missiles were housed.

Missiles were stored in pits, as opposed to missile silos that housed and launched intercontinental ballistic missiles (ICBMs). The missiles were readied for launch through an elevator and rail system that ferried missiles around the launch area. As with most military occupations, only those with clearance at the launch site traveled and worked at that portion of the Nike missile base. Those men residing on base would still live alongside their fire control counterparts as well as those serving as barbers, military police, cooks and others who were in a service capacity. Both sections included Command of Quarters, and the missile area had a sleeping area as well for those assigned as needed.

Two weeks out of every year, the men would travel to White Sands Proving Grounds Test Range in New Mexico to demonstrate their aptitude on the missile systems. The White Sands Proving Ground was where Wernher von Braun and other scientists of Hitler's Nazi Germany war machine were placed in secrecy in 1945. Operation Paperclip scoured Germany for potential scientists of use for the United States after the Second World War ended and used their expertise in building not only the U.S. rocket and satellite program but also the space program that would help found NASA in 1958. The Soviets also sought these men with expertise, sending not only scientists and technicians but also the entire manufacturing systems. In the United States, it was the expertise of these and other scientists that helped defeat the Soviet Union in the race to the moon.

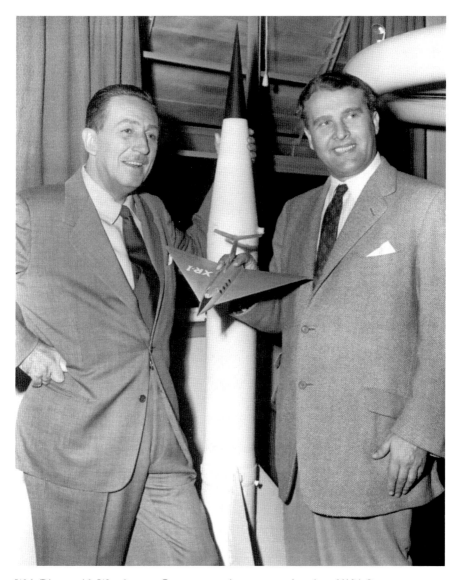

Walt Disney with Wernher von Braun promoting space exploration. *NASA Commons.*

First-generation Nike missiles were the Nike Ajax, which were conventional warheads that would soon be replaced with the Nike Hercules. The Nike Hercules missile was outfitted with a nuclear warhead, each with the strength of similar size and power of those dropped on Hiroshima and Nagasaki in Japan during the end of the Second World War. Nike Zeus, the third-generation system, was envisioned to become the answer

Lorton, Virginia Nike Ajax Missile Site in 1955. *Library of Congress.*

to anti-ballistic missile defenses after the USSR placed an emphasis on ICBMs. Sergei Khrushchev noted that his father, Nikita, was putting more emphasis on intercontinental long-range ICBMs in the late 1950s. With the focus on ICBMs by both sides of the Cold War stalemate, the Nike missile sites were rendered ineffective against that type of warfare weapon. Although the Nike system was eventually phased out and rendered obsolete in the United States, South Korea is one of the few places in the world where Nike sites have still been active in the twenty-first century. The Nike concept technology eventually evolved into the creation of the Patriot missile systems, which have been deployed in warfare in such places as the Middle East in recent decades.

VIRGINIA'S NIKE MISSILE SYSTEMS

Missile defense was a necessity in Virginia given the nearby location of the capital of the United States, Washington, D.C. It was and continues to function as the seat of the nation's elected and bureaucratic decision-makers, in addition to many military bases and defense-related contractors, research and development. In the event a third world war had broken out between the Soviet Union and United States during the Cold War, these institutions in Washington, D.C., and Virginia clearly would have been at the top of the list of military and civilian targets.

LIST OF NIKE MISSILE LOCATIONS IN VIRGINIA

Designation of the Nike systems included the first letter of the city or group the bases belonged to. Thus, the letter N stood for Norfolk and W for Washington, D.C. In total, there were eleven bases designated for Virginia/ Washington, D.C. An additional sixteen were located in the Maryland/ Washington, D.C. group of bases that are not listed in this book.

Below are the designations, city locations and current status as of this writing. As the Nike missile systems were dismantled, the idea was to offer these sites back to their communities for redevelopment and recreational purposes, such as city parks. That was not always the case in reality, as many bases around the country were eventually sold to private interests for housing, commercial and manufacturing development or continued in a military capacity.[1]

N - 52 Norfolk	Deep Creek Portsmouth	1955–1974 Chesapeake Alternative School
N - 85 Norfolk	Denbigh/ Patrick Henry	1955–1974 Peninsula Airport Commission
N - 25 Norfolk	Fort Story	1957–1971 Army Amphibious Training Site
N - 02 Norfolk	Fort Hill	1955–1963 Fort Monroe Training and Doctrine Command

N - 93 Norfolk	Hampton/ Spiegleville	1955–1963 U.S. Army Reserve Center
N - 36 Norfolk	Kempsville	1955–1964 City of Virginia Beach Parks and Recreation
N - 63 Norfolk	Nansemond/ Suffolk	1955–1964 USAR Center/Bennett's Creek Park
N - 75 Norfolk	Smithfield Carrolton	1955–1961 Isle of Wright County Park
W - 74 Washington	Fairfax/ Pohick	1954–1963 Fairfax County Ownership
W - 83 Washington	Herndon/ Drainsville	1954–1962 Defense Mapping Agency/Fairfax County
W - 64 Washington	Lorton	1954–1958 District of Columbia Minimum Security Prison

NIMBY: NOT IN MY BACKYARD

According to Nike veterans, there was never any official mention that the sites contained nuclear-equipped missiles until after the U.S. Army closed down these bases. Depending on the base, at any given time during their presence, there were about thirty missiles with twelve nuclear warheads ready to be placed on top of the delivery systems. Recalling that each was equivalent to those dropped on Japan during the Second World War should humble the reader considering the amount of firepower on standby in case of war. In the 1950s and early 1960s, Nike missile veterans recalled being welcomed in communities. It was not until the Vietnam War escalated that the resistance to war and these defensive missile systems took full force around the country. By the time the 1960s ended, the Nike systems had been used as a bargaining chip in the Strategic Arms Limitation Talks (SALT) that capped nuclear warheads for both the United States and Soviet Union. As mentioned prior, these systems were expensive to maintain and unnecessary against what evolved into an ICBM threat between the two superpowers. Thus, the Nikes fell out of favor, troop forces were reallocated and missile bases shut down.

DEMISE OF THE NIKE MISSILE SYSTEMS IN THE UNITED STATES

The Nike missile sites around the country were largely shut down by 1971 under terms of the SALT. A Nike Zeus missile was in development for years as a solution and deterrent to the ICBMs. But the Zeus was never fully deployed, falling out of favor for the Patriot missile in later years. Also factoring into the Nike missile demise was that as the Vietnam War assumed more manpower and resources, shutting down the Nike systems was an efficient decision to close the bases outright.

2

THE COLD WAR AND THE RACE TO SPACE

SPUTNIK, THE SPACE RACE
AND THE FOUNDING OF NASA AT LANGLEY

The significance of the Sputnik program in the Soviet Union cannot be underestimated. The Soviet Union was well aware the U.S. Air Force had at its disposal long-range bombers that could fly a nuclear payload from bases in England, West Germany, Turkey, South Korea, Japan and others into all corners of the Soviet Union. As the U.S. spy planes came online, Soviet Premier Nikita Khrushchev was absolutely livid about having American U-2 spy planes flying over the Soviet Union at nearly seventy thousand feet as well. The Soviet air defense sent MIGs scrambling to intercept the U-2, but they were no match for the lightning-fast American spy planes. The U-2 missions were a means to photograph Soviet military installations, troop strength, shipyards, missile sites and atomic testing sites and glean other significant information to keep an edge in the Cold War.

When the Soviet rocket program under Sergei Korolev and other engineers took shape after the Second World War, Nikita Khrushchev found an apparent fascination with rockets and ballistic missiles. Korolev's role with the Soviet Union was so secretive he was considered a man with no name, purposely unknown to the outside world to keep the Soviet space and rocket program a secret. Nikita's son Sergei Khrushchev, an accomplished engineer in his own right, reminisced about a meeting with Korolev displaying a world map with the distance missiles could travel into

Sputnik Satellite. *Russian News Agency.*

Soviet Space Exhibit in Moscow, 1959. *Library of Congress.*

enemy territory. Great Britain and France could equally be destroyed and conquered with five to nine missiles.[2]

Sergei Khrushchev also shared that his father not only embraced a solution to altering the power of missile development but was also attracted to the cost-effectiveness of ballistic missiles to close the gap of American air and nuclear superiority. Due to overwhelming costs, and having fallen technologically behind the Americans in a key military aerospace area, the Soviet Union could not develop a bomber program to match the United States. In its stead, Khrushchev raced to pull ahead in the development of intercontinental ballistic missiles. Designing new rockets and spacecraft to gain an edge in the superiority of space became a top objective. As far as the Americans were concerned at the time, the United States was so far advanced in air superiority and nuclear capabilities that the budget for satellites was merely $88,000 in 1954. The Sputnik launch in 1957 served as a wake-up call.

An ancillary effect of ICBMs was the closure of the many surface-to-air Nike missile sites around the United States, including those in Virginia. Nike missiles were tasked with patrolling the skies for enemy Soviet bombers. Washington, D.C., and Virginia military bases and ammunition plants such as Radford would be targeted by enemy bombers, traveling over the polar regions in route to drop their nuclear payloads on U.S. targets. With the rise of ICBMs and the underwhelming test performance of missile interceptors such as the Nike Zeus, the Nike sites were deemed too costly and obsolete for future Cold War conflict and shut down as part of the SALT (Strategic Limitations Arms Talks) in 1970. (See chapter 1 for more information.)

PIVOTAL MOMENT OF SPUTNIK

Nikita Khrushchev's gamble on space paid off on October 4, 1957, when the Soviet Union successfully launched Sputnik. After several years in development, Sputnik was launched as part of the International Geophysical Year (IGY) July 1, 1957, to December 31, 1958. The period was designed to foster more cooperation in the world's efforts to understand the sciences. Both the United States and the Soviet Union pledged to launch satellites during the IGY. Not to be outdone, each side would use the occasion as not only a diplomatic show of goodwill but also a test of their military capabilities.

The first Sputnik certainly did not warrant first prize in a beauty contest. The world's first successful artificial satellite launched into outer space could accurately be described as a 183-pound metal sphere the size of a basketball with an attached radio antenna. How it looked, however, was not at the top of Sergei Korolev's concerns. Korolev, who was plucked from a Siberian work camp in the Soviet gulag system in 1939, went on to direct the Soviet rocket and satellite program. Korolev insisted that Sputnik be a sphere; when covered with a polished aluminum material, the satellite would be seen in the upper recesses of the atmosphere.

After being successfully launched on Vostok rockets, the Sputnik satellite sent a series of beeps through four radio antennas that could be tracked and heard with ease with the correct equipment. One needed only a shortwave or ham radio to track the satellite as it passed overhead transmitting signals. Sputnik did so for nearly three weeks before the batteries wore out. Sputnik continued in orbit until January 1958, when the satellite malfunctioned and burned up in the atmosphere.

The United States Department of Defense watched with unease and concern and immediately responded to the ensuing political furor by approving funding for another U.S. satellite project to compete with the Vanguard satellite program. As a simultaneous alternative to Vanguard, which failed miserably on the launchpad in 1957, Wernher von Braun and his Army Redstone Arsenal team began work on the Explorer project. Explorer I would launch successfully in January 1958. This successful launch allowed the United States to keep up in the Space Race and save face by launching a satellite as promised during the International Geophysical Year.

Needless to say, the Sputnik launch ushered in not only a new era of scientific discovery, wonder and amazement but also a hereunto unforeseen fear of the Cold War consequences. Sputnik's presence in space caused alarm all over the United States and fostered an innovative approach to federalizing education, highlighting the need for science, math and engineering in American school systems. As the Space Race progressed, superiority in conquering the heavens had a direct implication on intercontinental ballistic missiles carrying nuclear payloads to the opposing forces of each country. The Sputnik satellite, although crude in design compared to technology today, covered nearly every habitable place on Earth during its orbit. Thus, fear resulted, since there was no place to hide from the reach of the Soviet's appearance of technological edge and potential military reach. It was therefore imminent to put necessary resources into finding such a way to get the upper hand in the Space Race on the part of the United States.

The most significant reaction in the United States was the National Aeronautics and Space Act in 1958, which resulted in the creation of NASA (National Aeronautics and Space Administration) to govern America's entry into space.

FOUNDING OF NASA IN LANGLEY

The Space Race was not the beginning of an interest in aviation in Langley, Virginia. Even though the Wright brothers had been the first to make a powered airplane flight in 1903, by the beginning of World War I in 1914, the United States lagged behind Europe in airplane technology. In order to catch up, Congress founded the National Advisory Committee for Aeronautics (NACA) on March 3, 1915, as an independent government agency reporting directly to the president.[3] As late as 1937, many prominent aviation legends, including Orville Wright, lent their credentials and advised this governing organization. The youngest member at the time was Charles Lindbergh, who first flew nonstop solo over the Atlantic from New York City to Paris.[4]

During the Second World War, Langley tested planes like the P-51 Mustang in the nation's first wind tunnel built for full-size aircraft. The changes made to warplanes such as the P-51 decreased fuel use and increased speeds—a combination that helped win the war. As Langley engineers pushed the aeronautics envelope after the Second World War, they partnered with the military on the Bell X-1, an experimental aircraft that would fly faster than the speed of sound. Then Air Force Captain Chuck Yeager piloted the X-1 into history, becoming the first person to break the sound barrier.

As the Cold War intensified and the Korean peninsula brought East and West into armed conflict in 1950, NACA devoted increased time and research to missile technology. It was responsible for developing the tactics and designs for the reentry of space vehicles. Initially, the focus was on missile warheads, but NACA later looked to the possibility of crewed vehicles. NACA expanded once again, adding a site for launching rocket-propelled airplane models for high-speed tests at Wallops Island, Virginia.

NACA also developed a plan that called for a blunt-body spacecraft that would reenter with a heat shield, a worldwide tracking network and dual controls that would gradually give the pilot of the craft greater control. All of these would become part of the space program, but not under NACA.

NASA Langley full-scale wind tunnel. *Library of Congress.*

The National Advisory Committee for Aeronautics was absorbed by NASA as it began official operations on October 1, 1958. This new organization began with eight thousand employees, an annual budget of $100 million, three major research laboratories—Langley Aeronautical Laboratory, Ames Aeronautical Laboratory and Lewis Flight Propulsion Laboratory—and two smaller test facilities. NASA would also soon include the Naval Research Laboratory in Maryland, the Jet Propulsion Laboratory managed by the California Institute of Technology for the Army and the Army Ballistic Missile Agency in Huntsville, Alabama, where Wernher von Braun's team of engineers was engaged in the development of large rockets. NASA created other centers, and today it has ten located around the country.

After the sound barrier was broken by Captain Yeager, researchers went back to work in Langley wind tunnels to reach higher speeds. Follow-on high-speed research would extend the reach of American aeronautics into the once-thought-impractical supersonic and hypersonic fields. By 1959, the X-15 would rocket to hypersonic speeds, traveling five times faster than sound, paving the way for manned spaceflight. Data gathered during X-15 flights directly contributed to the creation of the U.S. space program.

FIRST MAN INTO SPACE

The Soviet Sputnik program continued in earnest and succeeded at a high rate. As a consequence of the successful launch with Laika, a dog, and test launches with other stray dogs, the Soviet Sputnik II mission achieved a scientific foundation of life in space, as the first human to orbit the Earth would be launched from an advanced Vostok rocket a year later. Yuri Gagarin, Soviet cosmonaut, became humanity's first orbital passenger on April 12, 1961. It further cemented the Soviets' position as leading the charge into space. Unlike the Soviets, the Americans favored sending primates over dogs to test the effects on creatures as a precursor to sending a man into space.

On a peculiar yet understandably superstitious note, Yuri Gagarin was said to have started a tradition among cosmonauts. Before he became the first man in space in April 1961, Yuri Gagarin asked the bus driver to stop on the route to the launchpad and urinated against the right-hand back

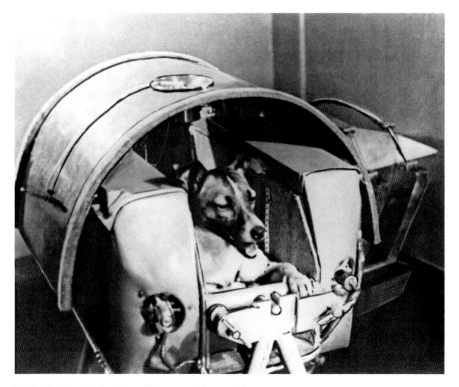

Laika the dog, Soviet Space Program. *Library of Congress.*

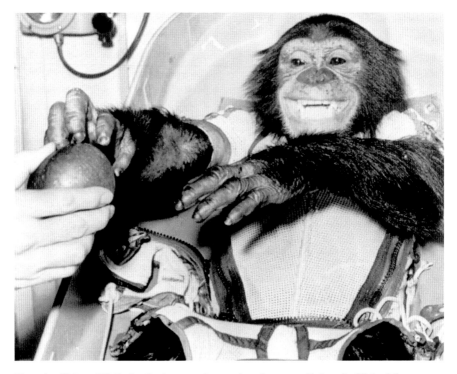

Ham the Chimp. While the Soviets tested stray dogs for space flights, the United States chose chimpanzees. *NASA Commons.*

tire of the bus. This act became a tradition for all cosmonauts traveling into space. The first woman in space, Valentina Tereshkova, continued this tradition: female cosmonauts brought vials of their urine to splash on the wheel.[5]

To push forward in the Space Race, the United States instituted the Mercury program to put a man in space in 1958. Twenty-three days after cosmonaut Yuri Gagarin's orbital flight, Alan Shepard Jr. became the first American and second man in space. Designated Freedom 7, it was the first flight of an American rocket with a human on board. The objectives of the flight were to complete a space flight experience, allow man to be a functional unit during space flight and recover the astronaut and spacecraft. The Mercury capsule lacked a window through which Shepard, who reached a G-Force of six, could view his surroundings. A periscope did allow him views of the outside during the pre-launch and weightless phases of the mission, however, during this fifteen-minute flight into space. After splashdown, the Mercury capsule and its pilot were returned by helicopter

Soviet cosmonaut Yuri Gagarin, first man in space, in 1961. *European Space Agency.*

to the aircraft carrier USS *Lake Champlain*. Three weeks after the first successful manned mission, President John F. Kennedy addressed Congress and set the nation's sights on a goal to send a man successfully to the Moon and back.[6]

The Space Race intensified so dramatically during the Cold War that even the terminology of what to call these space men was debated between East and West. An ongoing discussion began at NASA between *astronauts* and *cosmonauts*. Deputy administrator Hugh Dryden wanted to name U.S. travelers in space cosmonauts, the term that also applied to Russian spacemen. He felt that *cosmos* was more applicable to space travel than just the term used for stars (or "astro"). However, while he made a clear point, he was outvoted by his peers.[7]

PROJECT GEMINI

Gemini 3 was the first crewed Earth-orbiting spacecraft of the Gemini series. It was piloted by astronauts Virgil "Gus" Grissom and John Young, with the primary objective of demonstrating the crewed qualifications of the Gemini spacecraft, including evaluation of the two-man Gemini design, the worldwide tracking network, the orbit attitude and maneuver system (OAMS), the control of reentry flight path and landing point, spacecraft systems and spacecraft recovery. Secondary objectives included evaluation of flight crew equipment, effects of low-level launch vehicle oscillations (POGO) on the crew and performance of three experiments and obtaining photographic coverage from orbit.

The Gemini program was designed as a bridge between the Mercury and Apollo programs, primarily to test equipment and mission procedures in Earth orbit and to train astronauts and ground crews for future Apollo missions. The general objectives of the program included long-duration flights in excess of the requirements of a lunar landing mission; rendezvous and docking of two vehicles in Earth orbit; the development of operational proficiency of both flight and ground crews; the conduct of experiments in space; extravehicular operations; active control of reentry flight path to achieve a precise landing point; and onboard orbital navigation. Each Gemini mission carried two astronauts into Earth orbit for periods ranging from five hours to fourteen days. The program consisted of ten crewed launches, two un-crewed launches and seven target vehicles, at a total cost of approximately $1.3 million.[8]

PROJECT APOLLO

The singular achievement of NASA during its early years involved the human exploration of the Moon: Project Apollo. Apollo became a NASA priority on May 25, 1961, when President John F. Kennedy announced, "I believe that this nation should commit itself to achieving the goal, before this decade is out, of landing a man on the Moon and returning him safely to Earth." As a direct response to Soviet successes in space, Kennedy used Apollo as a high-profile effort for the United States to demonstrate to the world its scientific and technological superiority over its Cold War adversary.

In response to the Kennedy decision, NASA was consumed with carrying out Project Apollo and spent the next eleven years doing so. This effort required significant expenditures, costing $25.4 billion over the life of the program, to make it a reality. Only the building of the Panama Canal rivaled the size of the Apollo program as the largest nonmilitary technological endeavor ever undertaken by the United States to date. Moreover, only the Manhattan Project was comparable in a wartime setting.

Apollo 7 was the first crewed flight of the Apollo spacecraft, with astronauts Walter Schirra Jr., Donn Eisele and Walter Cunningham on board. The primary objectives of the Earth orbiting mission were to demonstrate Command and Service Module (CSM), crew, launch vehicle and mission support facilities performance and to demonstrate CSM rendezvous capability. Two photographic experiments and three medical experiments were planned.

The Apollo program included a large number of unmanned test missions and twelve crewed missions: three Earth orbiting missions (Apollo 7, 9 and Apollo-Soyuz), two lunar orbiting missions (Apollo 8 and 10), a lunar swing by (Apollo 13) and six Moon landing missions (Apollo 11, 12, 14, 15, 16 and 17). Two astronauts from each of these six missions walked on the Moon (Neil Armstrong, Edwin Aldrin, Charles Conrad, Alan Bean, Alan

Shepard, Edgar Mitchell, David Scott, James Irwin, John Young, Charles Duke, Gene Cernan and Harrison Schmitt), the only humans to have set foot on another solar system body. The final lunar landing, Apollo 17, took place on December 7, 1972, and no human has since been to the Moon.[9]

In 1968, the Apollo 7 and Apollo 8 missions to orbit the Earth and Moon were successful in testing the Apollo command module.[10] "That's one small step for man, one giant leap for mankind." Neil Armstrong uttered these famous words on July 20, 1969, when the Apollo 11 mission fulfilled Kennedy's challenge by successfully landing Armstrong and Edwin E. "Buzz" Aldrin Jr. on the Moon. Armstrong dramatically piloted the lunar module to the lunar surface with less than thirty seconds worth of fuel remaining. After collecting soil samples, taking photographs and doing other tasks on the Moon, Armstrong and Aldrin rendezvoused with their colleague Michael Collins in lunar orbit for a safe voyage back to Earth.

Mercury 7 Astronauts. On April 9, 1959, NASA introduced its first astronaut class, the Mercury 7. *Front row, left to right*: Walter M. Schirra Jr., Donald K. "Deke" Slayton, John H. Glenn Jr. and M. Scott Carpenter; *back row*: Alan B. Shepard Jr., Virgil I. "Gus" Grissom and L. Gordon Cooper Jr. *NASA Commons*.

As a response to the successful Apollo 11 lunar landing in July 1969, the Soviet government decided to develop the world's first civilian Earth orbital space station. On April 19, 1971, the Soviet Union placed into orbit Salyut, the world's first space station. Designed for a six-month on orbit operational lifetime, Salyut hosted the crew of Georgi T. Dobrovolsky, Vladislav N. Volkov and Viktor I. Patsayev for a then record-setting twenty-four-day mission. The flight ended tragically when the crew died due to the sudden depressurization of their Soyuz 11 spacecraft shortly before reentry into the Earth's atmosphere. The Soviet Union's other remarkable space achievement was the Mir Space Station, which would launch in 1986 before finally burning up in the atmosphere in 2001.[11]

Five more successful lunar landing missions followed for the United States. In 1975, NASA cooperated with the Soviet Union to achieve the first international human spaceflight, the Apollo-Soyuz Test Project (ASTP). This project successfully tested joint rendezvous and docking procedures for spacecraft from the United States and the Soviet Union. After being launched separately from their respective countries, the Apollo and Soyuz crews met in space and conducted various experiments for two days.[12]

SPACE SHUTTLE

After a gap of six years, NASA returned to human spaceflight in 1981 with the advent of the space shuttle. The shuttle's first mission took off on April 12, 1981, demonstrating that it could take off vertically and glide to an unpowered airplane-like landing. Sally K. Ride became the first American woman to fly in space when STS-7 (Space Transportation System) lifted off on June 18, 1983, setting another early milestone of the space shuttle and NASA program.

On January 28, 1986, a leak in the joints of one of two solid rocket boosters attached to the space shuttle *Challenger* orbiter caused the main liquid fuel tank to explode seventy-three seconds after launch, killing all seven crew members. The shuttle program was grounded for over two years, while NASA and its contractors worked to redesign the solid rocket boosters and implement management reforms to increase safety. On September 29, 1988, the shuttle successfully returned to flight.

TOWARD A PERMANENT HUMAN PRESENCE IN SPACE

The first effort in this area for the United States was the NASA Skylab program in 1973. After Apollo, NASA used its huge Saturn rockets to launch a relatively small orbital space workshop. There were three human Skylab missions, with the crews staying aboard the orbital workshop for twenty-eight, fifty-nine and then eighty-four days. In 1984, Congress authorized NASA to build a major new space station as a base for further exploration of space. By 1986, the design depicted a complex, large and multipurpose facility. In 1991, after much debate over the station's purpose and budget, NASA released plans for a restructured facility called Space Station Freedom.

Russia, which had many years of experience in long-duration human spaceflight, such as with its Salyut and Mir space stations, joined with the United States and other international partners in 1993 to build a joint facility that became known formally as the International Space Station (ISS). To prepare for building the ISS starting in late 1998, NASA participated in a series of shuttle missions to Mir, and seven American astronauts lived aboard Mir for extended stays.

THE SCIENCE OF SPACE

In addition to major human spaceflight programs, there have been significant scientific probes that have explored the Moon, the planets and other areas of our solar system. In particular, the 1970s heralded the advent of a new generation of scientific spacecraft. Two similar space crafts, Pioneer 10 and Pioneer 11—launched on March 2, 1972, and April 5, 1973, respectively—traveled to Jupiter and Saturn to study the composition of interplanetary space. Voyagers 1 and 2—launched on September 5, 1977, and August 20, 1977—conducted a "grand tour" of our solar system.

Over the years, NASA has continued to look for life beyond our planet. In 1975, NASA launched the two Viking spacecraft to look for basic signs of life on Mars; the spacecraft arrived on Mars in 1976 but did not find any indications of past or present biological activity there. In 1996, a probe from the Galileo spacecraft that was examining Jupiter and its moon Europa revealed that Europa may contain ice or even liquid water,

Space shuttle *Discovery* arrives at Dulles International Airport in 2012. *Library of Congress.*

thought to be a key component in any life-sustaining environment. NASA has also used radio astronomy to scan the heavens for potential signals from extraterrestrial intelligent life.[13]

The space shuttle program was bedeviled with another fatal accident with the explosion of the *Columbia* in 2003, with all seven astronauts aboard killed while descending from orbit over Texas and Louisiana. The shuttle program rebounded to continue multiple missions into the year 2011. At that time, costs of launching the space shuttle were largely attributed to budgetary concerns, and the program was discontinued. In 2012, space shuttle *Discovery*, active since 1984, was brought to the James S. McDonnell Space Hangar at the National Air and Space Museum's Steven F. Udvar-Hazy Center in Chantilly, Virginia.

3

THE NATIONAL RECONNAISSANCE OFFICE AND EVOLUTION OF SATELLITES

FROM EYES IN THE SKY TO EYES FROM SPACE

With the Space Race well underway with the Soviet Union's Sputnik launch in 1957, the United States was in a race to develop a solid photo-satellite reconnaissance system capable of peering into off-limits areas of the Soviet Union and Iron Curtain countries. Photo reconnaissance through the Corona program was initially launched as a temporary means to fill the intelligence void left by the anticipated suspension of U-2 overflights of the Soviet Union, which actually occurred after the downing of Francis Gary Powers's aircraft in May 1960. (See chapter 11 for more information.)

The National Reconnaissance Office (NRO) was established in 1960 after management problems and insufficient progress with the USAF satellite reconnaissance program. It was championed by the Polaroid Corporation's CEO Edwin H. "Din" Land and James R. Killian Jr., president of the Massachusetts Institute of Technology, who had already been involved in the Corona satellite program. Prior to the NRO, the United States Air Force and Central Intelligence Agency had shared responsibilities in developing the satellite reconnaissance program.[14]

Prior to the launch of reconnaissance satellites, the United States relied on and conducted its aerial reconnaissance missions with updated versions of B-47 and B-29 bombers from the Second World War. Teams of men would task these missions to test enemy air defenses and seek intelligence of enemy military strength. According to noted author James Bamford, forty military aircraft and nearly two hundred airmen lost their lives penetrating, or flying within short range, of Soviet airspace.[15] Because of these losses and the need for faster and higher-altitude reconnaissance missions, President Eisenhower authorized the U-2 program in 1954, followed by the A-12 Oxcart in 1959. Along with these high-altitude aircraft, and in later years the SR-71 Blackbird, an unparalleled advantage was maintained with photo reconnaissance satellites to oversee the Soviet Union, Warsaw Pact countries, the Middle East, China, active war zones and other areas of interest during the Cold War.

AMERICA'S FIRST RECONNAISSANCE SATELLITE

The first satellite reconnaissance and protection program, Samos, was actually begun as part of the WS-117L (Weapon System) satellite research and development of the U.S. Air Force in 1956.[16] The Air Force's WS-117L project included plans for a Signals Intelligence (SIGINT) payload, a payload in which film from an Imagery Intelligence (IMINT) payload would be scanned and transmitted to ground stations and a payload in which film would be returned to Earth via a reentry capsule. As the program experienced developmental challenges, and with the loss of the U-2 overflight operations in May 1960, that eventually left Corona as the nation's sole means of photo reconnaissance after its successful launch in August 1960.

Corona imagery showed that the Soviets had far fewer strategic missiles than was thought and dispelled the notion in the early 1960s of a "missile gap." This missile gap myth was perpetuated by John F. Kennedy during the presidential campaign of 1960. For the remainder of the Cold War, satellite IMINT, combined with SIGINT, consistently gave U.S. officials accurate estimates of how many missiles, bombers and submarines the Soviet Union had at any point in time. The expectation was to have Corona serve the nation for approximately two years before being replaced by the more sophisticated systems under development in the Air Force's Samos program. Instead, Corona served the nation for twelve years before being replaced by Hexagon, another technological initiative in the ever-expanding Cold War with the Soviet Union.

The successor satellite project named Hexagon began as a Central Intelligence Agency program with the first concepts proposed in 1964. The CIA's primary goal was to develop an imagery system with Corona-like ability to image wide swaths of the Earth but with higher resolution. Such a system would afford the United States even greater advantages monitoring the arms race that had developed with the nation's adversaries. Cooperation between the CIA and Air Force to build these systems became a major concern. These photo reconnaissance systems were an expensive undertaking. From 1971 to 1986, there were twenty launch attempts of the Hexagon by the NRO, with nineteen of those being successful. Ironically, it was the final launch, on April 18, 1986, that failed. That marked the end of the program, which cost a total of $3.262 billion (nearly $30 billion in 2023 dollars).[17]

By 1963, the Gambit system had already joined Corona and was providing significantly improved resolution for understanding details of those targets.[18] Both Gambit and Corona, followed by Hexagon, worked in tandem to provide better search and surveillance capabilities. In the case of Hexagon, images were taken at altitudes ranging from 90 to 200 miles. Each of the six-inch-wide frames of Hexagon film captured a swath of terrain that covered roughly 370 nautical miles on each pass over the Soviet Union and China. The cameras had a resolution of two to three feet. The satellite systems also required film to operate and assess, with the film canisters dropped into the atmosphere. They were retrieved midair by Lockheed C-130 military aircraft snagging the capsules' parachute. Eventually, these canisters made their way to Hawaii for analysis.

The technological advances in imagery reached optimal resolution and, as such, created more demand. As photo reconnaissance became a more reliable tool in intelligence gathering, it was highly sought after and capable of verifying strategic arms agreements with the Soviet Union. These programs also improved the nation's means for peering over the Iron Curtain that separated Western democracies from East European and Asian Communist countries. The inability to gain insight into vast "denied areas" required exceptional systems to understand threats posed by U.S. adversaries. Corona, as the first imagery satellite system, had paved the way to see into those areas.

VIRGINIA MILITARY BASES DURING THE COLD WAR

MARINE CORPS BASE QUANTICO

"Crossroads of the Marine Corps"

The commandant of the Marine Corps established Marine Barracks Quantico on May 14, 1917. Thousands would be trained in Quantico during World War I, including units of the much-lauded 4th Marine Brigade. In 1920, Marine Corps Schools was founded, and in the words of then Chief of Staff for Quantico Colonel Smedley D. Butler, their purpose was to "make this post and the whole Marine Corps a great university."

Beginning in 1935, the "Banana Wars" in the Caribbean tested new tactics and the equipment developed in Quantico. Tactical units that conducted new amphibious operations became the Fleet Marine Force (FMF) in 1935. The FMF, headquartered in Quantico, perfected equipment and techniques in anticipation of its future Pacific role. When the headquarters of the FMF left in 1941, Quantico's main task became the education of individual Marines, rather than the large unit training it had conducted in the past.

The amphibious warfare techniques developed in Quantico in the years before World War II made victory possible in the conflict's Pacific theater. Quantico also trained fifteen thousand lieutenants and numerous officers from other services who helped lead the United States to victory.

At the dawn of the Cold War era in 1947, Quantico Marines conceived of carrying troops from ship to shore by helicopter and formed a special squadron to test the idea: Marine Helicopter Squadron-1, commonly referred to now as HMX-1. The helicopter techniques they used there later proved invaluable during the Korean and Vietnam Wars.

On January 1, 1968, the base was redesignated the Marine Corps Development and Education Command (MCDEC) in the spirit of the command motto *Semper Progredi*, "Always Forward." During the summer of 1987, Quantico planners studied more efficient and streamlined ways in which MCDEC could ensure the Marine Corps of the future would be the best trained, led, disciplined and equipped fighting force on the planet. On November 10, 1987, the Marine Corps transitioned the Development and Education Command into the Marine Corps Combat Development Command (MCCDC).

Marine Corps University was also established in 1989 to provide the structure and policy for professional military education Corps-wide. Professional Military Education (PME) schools, which work alongside the university, include the Marine Corps War College, the School of Advanced Warfighting, the Command and Staff College, Expeditionary Warfare School, the Enlisted PME branch and the College of Distance Education and Training. As a result of the forward thinking of planners, it cemented Quantico's vital role in developing concepts, plans, doctrine, training and equipment for the twenty-first-century Marine Corps.[19]

LIFE ON BASE DURING THE COLD WAR

Quantico Corporal Cheryl Johnson served at the Marine Corps base from 1980 to 1984. The Cold War era shaped her thoughts on the world because of her work in proximity to Washington, D.C. She recalled boot camp at Parris Island in South Carolina as a challenging but growing experience as she entered Marine Corps training when she turned eighteen years old. She left a small town in Wisconsin due to not having many lucrative options there. She was from a big family with great support but decided to strike out on her own.

She reported to Arlington, Virginia Headquarters, which was then located in the Navy Annex Building. Her office faced Arlington National Cemetery. The building was eventually torn down in 2013. She would make her way to Quantico and work under Lieutenant General Hatch in charge at Roslyn after a brief stint at the Navy Annex Building.

One of the harsh realities of joining the Marines in 1980, or any branch of the military for that matter, was the public view of the U.S. military after "losing" the Vietnam War. The Marine Corps budget, like that of branches at the time, was extremely limited. In the 1970s, Marines were not sure they were going to get paid; the budgets were so austere. Headquarters was said to be out of so much money that staff had to be careful using the Marine Corps letterhead. In context, there were few word processors, so typewriters were the normal office equipment to type and draw up documents. Corporal Johnson said that plain white paper had to be the foundation until everything was correct. On many occasions, she would have her superiors look over anything typewritten. Oftentimes her superiors would not pay detailed mindfulness, and she would have to start over after finding simple grammatical errors. With such primitive computers available in 1980, the introduction of word processors was a step up. However, the staff had to use multiple floppy discs that had extremely limited memory. She recalled having to clear the floppy discs often to get documents printed.

Her military occupational specialty (MOS) entailed work through Research Development and Studies (RDS) that cooperated with the U.S. Army. Corporal Johnson transferred documents to Army divisions every few weeks from researching tanks, small arms and other weapons. Corporal Johnson assisted in selecting the M16 rifle as the new primary Marine Corps rifle, replacing the M14. The infrared film highlighting Light Armored Vehicle (LAV) firm's contractors were the main suppliers vying for the contracts.

Corporal Johnson recognized that infrared technology will find weaknesses in any weapon, so it was a priority for the Marine Corps to find a way to protect our military personnel by looking for low heat signature. Although she had a top security clearance, she eventually needed to upgrade for a North Atlantic Treaty Organization (NATO) clearance as her role expanded. The decisionmakers would need to go through the Security and Control Office to view documentation themselves or make the process easier by going through Cheryl and save time. Needless to say, they chose to upgrade her security clearance instead.

Corporal Johnson pointed out that women were not allowed to fire weapons to qualify on the range. She noticed Marine Corps recruiting posters that said, "Free a Man to Fight," which meant that, as a woman, she wasn't allowed to join in infantry combat. But office and support workers would assist in freeing up men for battle if she and other women joined. Costs were also a factor, since low budgets meant less ammunition for training. Rifle badge was eventually started for women in about 1982.

Barracks were extremely crowded for those stationed in Washington, D.C., and Marines were encouraged to live off base. She did not feel as if Washington, D.C., was that rough of a town at the time despite what she had heard before arriving. Tattoo parlors were hidden in alleyways, unlike today, where tattoos are not so taboo anymore. She received her first tattoo in the Marine Corps and was wise not to tell her mother. She was smart enough to have her tattoos hidden on her shoulder and hip, where the uniform covered them up. Nothing could show below the elbow due to short sleeves. Corporal Johnson relayed how she knew a fellow Marine who got a tattoo on his hand for the sole purpose of not being assigned mess duty. He lost rank and money and was reassigned, but it appears the decision was well worth it—he did not have to peel potatoes anymore.

Corporal Johnson worked with a remarkably diverse group of people. She recalled coworkers from Brooklyn, North Carolina and even the Bahamas. Many had different accents, and some had children. She had roommates such as an African American woman from Atlanta and neighbors with a family from Colombia. She had the distinction of never having to do laundry since going into the Marine Corps: they hired a maid for that. The Marine Corps, like other military branches, was a melting pot with no room for racism. The experience not only teaches respect for others, but practicing any kind of discrimination also could quickly affect your rank, condition of uniforms and paycheck. One of the best deals of being in the military for her was Veterans Administration (VA) loans. At the time, in the 1980s home loans were carrying 22 percent interest rates in most cases, which was extremely high. A VA loan had much better, affordable rates for those serving their country.

The drinking age on any military base was eighteen. Until the drinking age was changed to twenty-one in the States, the Marine Corps had its reputation precede itself when younger Marines would go drinking off base and cause trouble. Hence, the "old enough to vote—old enough to drink" argument was not looked on as a good one when used by civilians during her military experience. With recruitment low, it was not uncommon to find fellow coworkers who had experienced a "go to jail or join the Marine Corps" mentality. In other instances of accepting otherwise physically unqualified personnel, she had a coworker who was flat-footed but received a waiver.

In private life, Corporal Johnson hung out with the Navy and Army instead of gossiping on Monday morning with those in the Marine Corps.

She surmised those she was fraternizing with had a different work group and had less of a chance to affect her career negatively. In her off time with friends, she could have a few drinks for less than a dollar at the bar on base. In Georgetown, the bars were two or three times the cost, so it was more cost-effective.

IMPACT OF RONALD REAGAN PRESIDENCY

When Johnson enlisted in the Marine Corps, Jimmy Carter was president of the United States. By the time she arrived in Washington, D.C., Ronald Reagan was president. With morale low and public confidence and viewpoint of the military unsatisfactory, military officers wore civilian attire while in public. President Reagan decreed uniforms be worn, and morale and pride in being a member of the U.S. military rose again. President Reagan also wanted to win the Cold War and send the Soviet Union and Communism to the ash heap of history. Budgets were increased dramatically as a result. The Marine Corps would have plenty of ammunition and no need to worry about such minute details as paper hoarding for office workers. Johnson distinctly recalled when the Iranian hostages were released during Reagan's inauguration, within moments of him taking the oath of office.

BEIRUT BOMBING

In 1983, the Marine barracks in Beirut were attacked by a suicide bomber, killing 241 military personnel in their sleep. Among the dead were 220 Marines, 18 Navy and 3 United States Army. At least two deceased individuals were CIA officers. (See chapter 7 on the CIA for further information.) Research and Development Studies studied the attack by looking at the truck going through the gates. Corporal Johnson indicated it was up to the ambassadors to develop security at overseas bases. Civilians were sending letters and suggestions for help to protect troops, but Corporal Johnson was ordered not to answer any of the letters.

Corporal Johnson followed the Cold War even after her discharge at the age of twenty-two in 1984. She was very cognizant from a military standpoint on world affairs. She noted the Soviets put bombs in toys during their military occupations. This brutal method was aimed at kids so they would not have hands to shoot weapons at the Soviets in their occupied territories in Afghanistan. This action also acted as a way to neutralize the occupied civilians as children so they would not be able to overthrow the Soviet occupiers as adults.

On television, she watched the Soviet May Day parades, viewing tanks and planes going on seemingly forever to give the impression of the mighty size of their military. In reality, they changed the Vehicle Identification Number (VIN) and other markings after turning the corner while televising military vehicles to the world. All the while, the Soviets kept the same number of military vehicles and weapons systems in the parade. She is convinced that Ronald Reagan bankrupted the Soviet Union and helped destroy the Evil Empire. Corporal Johnson was appalled that Mikhail Gorbachev was named Man of the Decade by *Time* magazine in the 1980s.[20]

NAVAL STATION NORFOLK

Naval Station Norfolk serves as the headquarters and home port of the U.S. Navy's Fleet Forces Command. At the end of the Second World War, the United States had a massive naval industrial complex. With more than one hundred field establishments, including ammunition depots, ordnance plants and a "big gun" factory, the Navy Bureau of Ordnance had an enormous production base to count on. The effect of this postwar complex set the stage for the Navy's ability to project force for the United States throughout the Cold War era. Ushering in the nuclear age, the United States was poised to create and sustain a naval fleet that was unparalleled in both size and technology, marked by the launching of USS *Nautilus* in 1955, the world's first nuclear submarine.[21]

In 1948, Atlantic Fleet headquarters moved into spaces of the former U.S. Navy hospital in Norfolk, which is present-day Naval Support Activity (NSA) Hampton Roads. In the early 1950s, the North Atlantic Treaty Organization (NATO) decided to establish a new major command (Allied Command Atlantic) under the command of a four-star U.S. admiral with headquarters in Norfolk, Virginia. Since this was primarily a naval command responsible for allied defense of the North Atlantic, the decision was made to co-locate this organization with that of U.S. Atlantic Command and U.S. Atlantic Fleet to form a tri-hatted command structure.

As the base continued to be a major facility throughout the Cold War, it saw periods of massive expansion to accommodate larger ships and a rebuilt fleet in the 1970s and 1980s. During this period, the Navy continued to expand the base with the purchase of nearly 495 acres of land from the Norfolk and Western Railway at a cost of $17.4 million. The new $60 million construction program resulted in new piers along the waterfront, as well as beautification and improvements to Hampton Boulevard leading to the main gate.[22]

One of the most frightening times in world history came during the Cuban Missile Crisis in October 1962. Weighing military and diplomatic options, President John F. Kennedy made the decision to blockade Cuba. This decision was made in response to the Soviets building missiles on the island that were to threaten the United States just ninety miles off the coast of Florida. The Atlantic Fleet deployed USS *Enterprise* along with four other carriers, *Independence*, *Essex*, *Lake Champlain* and *Randolph*, in order to prevent Soviet vessels from reaching Cuba. U.S. ships were also tasked with inspecting Soviet ships arriving at and departing from Cuba.

A narrow escape between American and Soviet naval vessels occurred under already tense circumstances, barely averting certain doom. An American destroyer, USS *Beale*, began to drop depth charges on the *B-59*, a Soviet submarine armed with a nuclear weapon. The captain of the *B-59*, Valentin Savitsky, had no way of knowing that the depth charges were nonlethal "practice" rounds intended as warning shots to force the *B-59* to surface.

Beale was joined by other U.S. destroyers that piled in to pummel the submerged *B-59* with more explosives. The exhausted Savitsky assumed that his submarine was doomed and that a Third World War had broken out. He ordered *B-59*'s ten-kiloton nuclear torpedo to be prepared for firing. Its target was USS *Randolph*, the giant aircraft carrier leading the task force. Vasili Alexandrovich Arkhipov, a senior officer on board the Soviet submarine, chased down Savitsky and annulled the launch, saving potentially millions of lives in the process from a probable nuclear retaliation by the United States.[23]

After the Cuban Missile Crisis dissolved and Soviet ships retreated, emphasis was placed on nuclear ballistic missile submarines of the Atlantic Fleet. These submarines were tasked with deterring Soviet submarines and aircraft with patrols off the Atlantic coast. These submarines were originally outfitted with the Polaris 1-A, which was developed in 1960. The Trident missile systems upgraded the American fleet in 1980.[24]

At its height during the Cold War, Naval Station Norfolk was host to more than seventy tenant commands, including several carrier groups, carrier airborne early warning wings, helicopter sea control wings and Naval Air Reserve units. In addition, the station rendered support in photography, meteorology and electronics to the fleet commands of the Hampton Roads naval community.[25]

Beginning in the 1960s, Defense Secretary Robert McNamara started shifting production away from the Navy-owned shipyards and toward private establishments like those at Newport News, Virginia. Few naval facilities were actually closed due to this change, but the shift represented a fundamental reevaluation of the naval shipbuilding business. By the late 1960s, the focus was on modernization of existing facilities, bringing shipyards and manufacturing plants into a more modern state, this being set off by problems that were manifesting themselves during the conflict in Vietnam. The program of modernization reached its peak in a period between 1965 and 1971, when the Navy spent a total of $300 million on improvements. At this time, though, the manufacturing base began to contract, caused by fundamental shifts in U.S. defense manufacturing policy. The DOD adopted a "short war" scenario, based on the belief that wars would be short and intense, either quickly defusing or escalating into an exchange of strategic nuclear weapons. Instead, the DOD opted to move toward reduced numbers of facilities running at peak levels in general. This coincided with reduced defense spending, leading to things such as a fleet reduction from over one thousand ships to fewer than five hundred between the 1960s and 1980s. By the 1980s, the Navy was left with only a single shipyard in the country, Newport News Shipbuilding and Drydock Company (Newport News Shipbuilding), which could fulfill the requirements of the Navy's fleet. The Reagan buildup of the late 1980s did help to alleviate this somewhat, especially in the Navy, with the announcement of the six-hundred-ship Navy. This buildup helped leave the U.S. Navy on a strong footing as it exited the Cold War, despite difficulties that would continue to manifest through the 1990s.

RADFORD AMMUNITION PLANT

The Radford Army Ammunition Plant (RFAAP) is located in the mountains of southwest Virginia in Pulaski and Montgomery Counties. RFAAP consists of two noncontiguous units: the Main Manufacturing Area and the New River Unit. The Main Manufacturing Area is located approximately five miles northeast of the city of Radford, Virginia, which is approximately ten miles west of Blacksburg and forty-seven miles southwest of Roanoke. The New River Unit is located about six miles west of the Main Manufacturing Area, near the town of Dublin.

RFAAP lies in one of a series of narrow valleys typical of the eastern range of the Appalachian Mountains. Oriented in a northeast-southwest direction, the valley is approximately twenty-five miles long, eight miles in width at the southeast end and narrowing to two miles at the northeast end. RFAAP lies along the New River in the relatively narrow northeastern corner of the valley. The New River divides the Main Manufacturing Area into two sections, with the "Horseshoe Area" being within the meander of the river. Construction at the current RFAAP began in 1940, as Congress saw a need to increase ammunition production facilities due to anticipated involvement in the Second World War.

RFAAP initially consisted of two areas—a smokeless powder plant (Radford Ordnance Works) and a bag manufacturing and loading plant for artillery, cannon and mortar projectiles (New River Ordnance Works). Each operated separately through 1945. That year, the Radford Ordnance Works was renamed "Radford Arsenal" and assumed New River Ordnance Works as a sub post. In 1950, New River Ordnance Works (now known as the New River Unit) became an integral part of the Radford Arsenal and remained so as the arsenal was renamed "Radford Ordnance Plant" in 1961 and RFAAP in 1963.

RFAAP is still manufacturing propellants, its primary mission since 1941. The plant has also produced TNT on an intermittent basis since 1968. RFAAP's TNT facilities have been on standby since the mid-1980s. The working population at RFAAP varies greatly with mission requirements.

Radford Ammunition Plant had its share of casualties supporting the Cold War. In February 1985, according to a *Washington Post* article, a five-thousand-pound batch of nitroglycerin exploded at the plant, killing one worker, leaving another one missing and presumed dead and turning the building where they worked into a half-acre crater.[26] Up to that point, in fifteen years there had been nine major explosions at Radford, the nation's largest military munitions plant, resulting in seven deaths, more than 115 injuries and millions of dollars in damage. Army officials stated that the Radford plant had a safety record unmatched in the munitions industry. "The arsenal," as it is called in this small town on the edge of the Blue

Ridge Mountains forty miles southwest of Roanoke, was this rural region's largest employer at the time, providing jobs for four thousand at the time of explosion.[27]

LANGLEY AIR FORCE BASE

Originally designated the 633rd Combat Support Group, Langley Air Force Base was established and activated on March 14, 1966, and organized on April 8, 1966. It was originally assigned to the 13th Air Force as part of the Pacific Air Forces at Pleiku Air Base, South Vietnam, and later at Andersen Air Force Base, Guam. During the Vietnam War, airmen of the 633rd ABW participated in numerous campaigns, air offensives and Operations Arc Light, Bullet Shot and Linebacker. On October 1, 1989, the wing aligned under the 13th Air Force and activated at Andersen AFB, Guam, becoming the host unit, providing services for various tenant units. This marked the

Langley AFB in 1959. *National Archives.*

transfer of Andersen AFB's control from Strategic Air Command to PACAF. Personnel began shipping more than 37,000 tons of munitions to forces in the Persian Gulf during Operations Desert Shield and Desert Storm. More than 30,000 tons went by sealift, and more than 2,200 troops and 2,200 tons of cargo were processed aboard 200 aircraft.[28]

NAVAL WEAPONS STATION YORKTOWN

Naval Weapons Station Yorktown was acquired for the Navy by a presidential proclamation on August 7, 1918, by President Woodrow Wilson and was at the time the largest naval installation in the world, with its land area covering about twenty square miles. In 1932, it became known as Navy Mine Depot in recognition of expanded ordnance support. With the Cold War in tow in 1958, and on the station's fortieth anniversary, the name was changed to Naval Weapons Station Yorktown. Naval Weapons Station Yorktown has hosted forty tenant commands, including the Navy Munitions Command Atlantic, the Naval Ophthalmic Support and Training Activity, the Marine Corps Security Force Regiment, Navy Expeditionary Logistics Support Group, Naval Expeditionary Medical Support Command, Navy Cargo Handling Battalion One and nineteen departments.[29]

WARRENTON TRAINING CENTER

Warrenton Training Center (WTC) is a classified U.S. government communications complex created in June 1951 as a function of the Federal Relocation Arc. The facility was constructed of fortified underground bunkers designed to withstand nuclear attack and the ensuing fallout. The purpose was to provide a facility where the government could continue to function in the aftermath of a nuclear attack on the United States. The publicly presented reason for construction of the Warrenton Training Center during this time was as a communications training school for the Department of Defense.

WTC continues to serve multiple roles, most notably as a Central Intelligence Agency signals intelligence facility, numbers station and communications laboratory. The center also houses at least one underground relocation bunker that serves U.S. continuity of government purposes and is a communications and signals intelligence training school for various federal departments and agencies, including the CIA, National Security Agency (NSA), Department of Defense and Department of State. Additionally, it is a relay facility for the Department of State's Diplomatic Telecommunications Service. The U.S. Army administers WTC on behalf of the government.

In 1973, the facility command was transferred to the Department of the Army and was to be directly commanded by the Army Security Agency, the signals intelligence branch. During this time, the Warrenton Training Center was designated as the U.S. Army Training Group, Warrenton Training Center, and was subordinate to the National Security Agency. This system was kept in place until 1982, when the facility was rebranded to its original name and command was restored to the Department of Defense, with the Department of the Army acting as the administrative executive agent at the behest of the National Communication System.

Acting through the National Communication System—and after 2012 under the newly created Department of Homeland Security—the Warrenton Training Center was tasked with facilitating communication for the federal government in any situation. This includes anything ranging from natural disaster to full-scale nuclear attack by a hostile entity.

Station A continues to be used as a residential, training and administrative facility for multiple agencies, including the CIA and Department of State. Station B, the official headquarters of the Warrenton Training Center, includes multiple buildings and facilities such as underground bunkers. Facilities at Station B include equipment maintenance, communications training, electronics testing and a communications development laboratory. Station B is also home to the Brushwood Conference facility, which was built in the mid-1990s. Station C has been designated as a CIA numbers station and is tasked with transmitting coded signals to U.S. embassies and assets overseas. Station D is tasked with being a receiving point for high-frequency traffic for the CIA Office of Communications. Additionally, Station D plays host to a wide array of satellite communication facilities and serves as a core relay station for the region, relaying secure traffic for the Department of State's Diplomatic Telecommunications Service. The Warrenton Training Center remains a classified site, and in being such, access is limited to those stationed or employed there.[30]

VIRGINIA'S NIKE MISSILE SYSTEMS

Missile defense was a necessity in Virginia, as it is near to the location of the capital of the United States, Washington, D.C. It was and continues to function as the seat of the nation's elected and bureaucratic decisionmakers, in addition to its many military bases and defense-related contractors and research and development. In the event a third world war broke out between the Soviet Union and United States during the Cold War, these institutions in Washington, D.C., and Virginia clearly were at the top of the list of military and civilian targets.

LIST OF NIKE MISSILE LOCATIONS IN VIRGINIA

Designation of the Nike systems included the first letter of the city or group the bases belonged to. Thus, the letter *N* stood for Norfolk and *W* for Washington, D.C. In total there were eleven bases designated for Virginia/ Washington, D.C. An additional sixteen were located in the Maryland/ Washington, D.C. group of bases that are not listed in this book. (For more detailed information, see chapter 1.)

Below are the designations, city locations and current status as of this writing. As the Nike missile systems were dismantled, the idea was to offer these sites back to the communities for redevelopment and recreational purposes, such as city parks. That was not always the case in reality, as many bases around the country were eventually sold to private interests for housing, commercial and manufacturing development or continued in a military capacity. [31]

N - 52 Norfolk	Deep Creek Portsmouth	1955–1974 Chesapeake Alternative School
N - 85 Norfolk	Denbigh/ Patrick Henry	1955–1974 Peninsula Airport Commission
N - 25 Norfolk	Fort Story	1957–1971 Army Amphibious Training Site

N - 02 Norfolk	Fort Hill	1955–1963 Fort Monroe Training and Doctrine Command
N - 93 Norfolk	Hampton/ Spiegleville	1955–1963 U.S. Army Reserve Center
N - 36 Norfolk	Kempsville	1955–1964 City of Virginia Beach Parks and Recreation
N - 63 Norfolk	Nansemond/ Suffolk	1955–1964 USAR Center/ Bennett's Creek Park
N - 75 Norfolk	Smithfield Carrolton	1955–1961 Isle of Wright County Park
W - 74 Washington	Fairfax/Pohick	1954–1963 Fairfax County Ownership
W - 83 Washington	Herndon/Drainsville	1954–1962 Defense Mapping Agency/ Fairfax County
W - 64	Washington Lorton	1954–1958 District of Columbia Minimum Security Prison

BOMARC MISSILE SYSTEMS IN VIRGINIA

The BOMARC (Boeing Michigan Aeronautical Research Center) IM-99 Weapon System was a surface-to-air SAM missile system developed by the U.S. Air Force for domestic air defense needs after the Second World War. The system was in direct competition with the U.S. Army's successful deployment of the Nike Ajax (later the Hercules weapons systems) around the United States. Since the Soviet Union decided to place an emphasis on ICBMs, the Air Force BOMARC were never deployed in the numbers of site proposals planned. Along with the Nike Missile systems, most of what were BOMARC operating sites, including the Langley system, were deactivated in the early 1970s.

The 22nd Air Defense Missile Squadron was activated in September 1959 at Langley Air Force Base, Virginia. All of its activities were aimed toward attaining "Operational Ready" status. Skilled technicians and support personnel were assigned; supply items were received, classified and stocked. Air Police personnel were trained to provide security and missile site facilities inspected for conformance with highest standards.

Included in the activation period was a three-month unit training phase at Hurlburt Field on the Gulf coast of Florida. The squadron then returned to its home station to assume its position in the Air Defense Network. The Air Defense Command unit was assigned to the Headquarters, Washington Air Defense Sector at Fort Lee, Virginia. Initially located on base, the 22nd later moved to the Oyster Point area near Highway 168 in Newport News, where the U.S. Army Corps of Engineers had completed a $5.5 million missile complex. Billeting and messing facilities for the squadron's personnel remained at Langley.

By late November 1960, the first two missiles had been delivered to the 110-acre Oyster Point BOMARC site for minor assembly and testing of components and systems. The missiles' ramjet engines, which had arrived earlier, were installed at that time. With a range of 250 miles, the 15,000-pound missile could be launched vertically from concrete shelters by means of a boost rocket. The squadron was inactivated in October 1972 and the BOMARC site transferred to the City of Newport News.[32]

THE FARM-CIA TRAINING AREA

Although never acknowledged by the U.S. government, Camp Peary is a military base near Williamsburg, Virginia. The base is the site of the Central Intelligence Agency's officer training grounds, as well as the Defense Intelligence Agency's Defense Clandestine Service. The site has been referred to as the "Farm" due to hogs being raised on the property during the Second World War. Camp Peary initially had shared usage from the U.S. Army, Navy and Marines for training over the years since its inception in 1942 during the Second World War. Military units being transferred to various locations on the Atlantic coast led to the CIA and Defense Intelligence Agency overseeing the property.

LIFE ON THE FARM

Although many of the activities on the site are kept quiet, some former officers have come forward over the years and discussed what takes place during the intense CIA training methods for use against enemies of the United States. According to James Olson, former CIA chief of counterintelligence and Moscow chief of station during the Cold War, surveillance detection is a fine art. "There's probably nothing we studied more at the Farm or during the Denied Area Course than how to do that."[33]

For Olson, a seasoned spy, the Denied Area Course involved advanced training at the Farm and a year of intense preparation where he was exposed to stressful situations he would face in the field: screaming, impossible deadlines and 24-7 surveillance among them. Olson and his wife, Meredith, also a CIA agent, even lived in a CIA-bugged apartment to mimic what life would be like in Soviet Russia, where the walls had ears and eyes. All the while, psychologists evaluated their every move: "Part of the objective of the training was to winnow out those that could not withstand the kind of pressure of operating under surveillance, under constant pressure, with no margin for error and the consequences of a mistake being literally fatal." Technical officers at the Farm also developed the ultimate mission simulation for Olson, using satellite imagery taken during the construction of an underground Russian cable so he could learn how to tap into it and gather intelligence. The Farm designed a piecemeal recreation of the Moscow manhole and the trench beneath it, along with alarms Olson might need to pass through and Russian padlocks he might need to pick. During a dry run, Olson dropped a knife. He bled profusely but carried on, only to flunk for leaving telltale blood at the simulated site. Eventually, however, Olson successfully completed his real-life Moscow mission.

VINT HILL FARMS STATION

While conducting their work during the Second World War, farmers working at Vint Hill noticed that they were intercepting messages in German on their radios. After alerting the U.S. Army, Vint Hill's greatest secret was discovered: the land sits on an extremely rare geological formation that serves as a long-range antenna, and the messages coming through the radio waves were direct from Berlin. By June 1942, the Army had purchased Vint

Hill from Mitchell Harrison, a businessman who bought the property in 1911. The site would become the country's newest listening post and named Monitoring Station No. 1.[34]

Vint Hill Farms Station was largely staffed by women from the Women's Army Corps, highly trained to understand and translate Morse code messages. Highly intelligent women with backgrounds in mathematics and foreign languages were recruited for these critical roles, and they were largely credited with providing the raw data they received to analysts. These messages would then be used to inform military decisions that were made and carried out overseas. Messages were intercepted and analyzed for more than a year before a huge break gave the United States the intelligence it needed to change the course of the war.

Vint Hill Farms Station contributed importantly to the Allied effort, especially with regard to the planning for the invasion of Europe in 1944 (D-Day). As described in more detail later, it was a radio monitor at Vint Hill who first intercepted a vitally important encoded message from the Japanese ambassador to Germany, Oshima Hiroshi, as it was transmitted from Berlin to Japan. The message, which described the German coastal defenses in western France, also confirmed Allied suspicions about Nazi defensive strategies and troop dispositions and thereby affected D-Day planning.[35]

After the Second World War, Vint Hill Farms Station remained an active Army base and served as a training outpost for cryptanalysts and radio operators. While the area remained quieter than wartime years, it served as a key role in the Cuban Missile Crisis in 1962. After a period of time when Vint Hill served as a research base, it was ultimately closed in 1997 when its military usefulness expired.

THE COLD WAR MUSEUM

Since 2011, The Cold War Museum has been located at Vint Hill, Virginia. The museum is situated on the grounds of the former Vint Hill Farms Station, also known as Monitoring Station No. 1, which was a top-secret Army signals intelligence base during the Second World War and the Cold War. The Cold War Museum was founded in 1996 by Francis Gary Powers Jr., son of the famed U-2 pilot, and John Welch to preserve Cold War history, honor Cold War veterans and educate future generations about the Cold War and its legacy.

The Cold War Museum collections are particularly strong in signals intelligence (SIGINT), image intelligence (IMINT), the history of Vint Hill during both World War II and the Cold War, Cold War Berlin, civil defense, atomic weapons, the Liberty and Pueblo incidents, Cold War cultural and Olympic competitions, Strategic Air Command, submarine detection (SOSUS), the Cuban Missile Crisis, the STASI (East German secret police) and Soviet and East German disinformation campaigns. Many of its artifacts are rare, and some are one-of-a-kind; many exhibits were created and donated by those who did the work.

THE PENTAGON: SYMBOL OF AMERICAN MILITARY MIGHT

The Pentagon was the brainchild of Army Brigadier General Brehon B. Somervell, who, in the early 1940s, pitched it as a temporary solution to the then War Department's critical shortage of space as the threat of joining the Second World War became imminent. The plan was approved, and on September 11, 1941, construction began, exactly sixty years before the September 11, 2001 terrorist attacks.[36] The land the Pentagon was first planned to be situated on was bordered on five sides by roads, so the architects designed a five-sided building. President Franklin Delano Roosevelt was worried putting the building at that location would interfere with the view of Washington from Arlington Cemetery, so he chose to move it to its present location but kept the five-sided design.

Colonel Leslie Groves, an Army Corps of Engineers officer, took charge of the Pentagon's construction in August 1941. He worked six days a week in his office in Washington. On Sundays, he would visit the project he felt most needed his personal attention. Groves later said of his time at the Pentagon that he was "hoping to get to a war theater so I could find a little peace." Instead, he was assigned to direct the Manhattan Project—America's effort to build an atomic bomb.[37]

The grounds and building went up in a stunning sixteen months. The building was officially completed in January 1943, thanks to the help of 1,000 architects and 14,000 tradesmen who worked three shifts around the clock. A staggering amount of materials was needed, including 435,000 yards of concrete, 43,000 tons of steel and 680,000 tons of sand and gravel. Wartime office space shortages meant that workers moved in before the

United States Pentagon. *Library of Congress.*

The Washington Monument and the United States Capitol can be seen from the Pentagon construction site. *Library of Congress.*

Progress made on the Pentagon construction site. *Library of Congress.*

Pentagon was fully finished. Construction finished on January 15, 1943, just sixteen months after it started. Speed costs money, however. Initially budgeted at $35 million, the final cost was $63 million, more than $900 million in today's money. The first tenants moved into the building in April 1942, several months before the building was finished.

The Pentagon continues to be one of the world's largest office buildings at about 6.5 million square feet, of which about half (or 3.6 million square feet) is used as offices. Approximately 23,000 military and civilian employees and about 3,000 non-defense support personnel work in the Pentagon. It has five sides, five floors above ground, two basement levels and five ring corridors per floor with over seventeen miles of corridors. The Pentagon includes a five-acre central plaza shaped like a pentagon

Pentagon building taking shape. *Library of Congress.*

and informally known as "ground zero," a nickname that originated during the Cold War on the presumption that it would be targeted by the Soviet Union at the outbreak of nuclear war. On September 11, 2001, American Airlines Flight 77 was hijacked and flown into the western side of the building, killing 189 people.[38]

5

WOODROW WILSON AND THE ORIGINS OF THE COLD WAR

PRESIDENT WOODROW WILSON

Although the Cold War is primarily associated with geopolitical realities between the United States and the Soviet Union after the Second World War, its origins are firmly rooted in the First World War. At the dawn of the twentieth century, America was ascending into a powerful nation, and the First World War cemented its status as a participant of that conflict. Tsarist Russia collapsed during the "war to end all wars" in 1917, only to be replaced by the Bolshevik Party with Vladimir Lenin, Joseph Stalin and others that would eventually morph into the Soviet Union. As president, Woodrow Wilson acquiesced to British pressure to send U.S. troops into the thick of the Russian Civil War, formulate the predecessor to the United Nations (League of Nations) and help pass domestic and wartime acts that would federalize and empower Washington, D.C. agencies throughout the twentieth century in the fight against Communism.

Wilson was born on December 28, 1856, in Staunton, Virginia. His father, Joseph Ruggles Wilson, was a Presbyterian minister who had moved to Virginia from Ohio. Apparently dyslexic from childhood, Woodrow Wilson did not learn to read until after he was ten and never became a rapid reader. Nevertheless, he developed enthusiastic interests in politics and literature. After graduation from Princeton in 1879, Wilson made his way back to Virginia to study law at the University of Virginia with the hope that law would lead to politics. After modernizing Princeton University, he was encouraged to run for governor of New Jersey. Just two years later, he ran for president of the United States and won a three-way election with main challengers Theodore Roosevelt and William Howard Taft.[39] Eugene Debs, running as the Socialist Party of America nominee, managed to garner 6 percent of the vote.

One of Woodrow Wilson's lasting legacies was centralizing power in Washington, D.C. President Wilson's progressive initiatives shifted the balance of power between the states and the federal government in a way that usurps the original Constitution to this day. Under his successful proposals with Congress, the U.S. government made several major monetary changes, beginning with the implementation of a federal income tax titled the Revenue Act of 1913. Income tax was not a novel idea but, along with passage of the Sixteenth Amendment, strengthened the federal government's role in matters of taxation.[40]

The Federal Reserve System and Federal Trade Commission Act of 1914, which created the Federal Trade Commission, a major agency overseeing business practices, were related to the new monetary policies of the federal government by Wilson. Coupled with the passage of the Seventeenth Amendment, which allowed for direct elections of senators rather than appointment by state legislatures, a national centralized government was on its way to building more power that continues its dominance over a century later.[41]

These monetary events as defined through taxation allowed for a direct source of revenue through which future wars would be financed and waged throughout the twentieth century, including the Cold War. In addition, this shift in philosophy would redefine the nature of the individual, the states and federal government. In that same vein, the roles of governance in this era were mirrored by Bolshevik Russia and Weimar Germany, each with dire consequences after Wilson's failure at Versailles and his Fourteen Points for peace after the First World War.

Although major domestic victories were key to Woodrow Wilson's first term, foreign affairs would come to dominate the second term. Acts of aggression with Pancho Villa in Mexico in 1916 and eventual entry into the First World War in 1917 would be defining moments of his presidency. Wilson pleaded to stay neutral in the war and unsuccessfully sought to negotiate a peaceful settlement between the Axis and Allies. However, with the sinking of the *Lusitania* in 1915, German war interference with Mexico and further U-boat terror by the Germans sinking U.S. maritime ships finally drove Wilson to ask Congress for a declaration of war in 1917. The Selective Service Act, or military draft, was signed into law as well, in order to conscript troops into war service in 1917.

QUELLING DISSENT AT HOME

With the war underway, President Wilson pushed for new laws that potentially criminalized core First Amendment speech. Congress passed the Espionage Act shortly after the United States entered the war. The act made it a crime to convey information intended to interfere with the war effort. This act would later be used to convict Julius and Ethel Rosenberg in 1951 during the Cold War. Later, the Sedition Act imposed harsh penalties for a wide range of dissenting speech, including language abusing the U.S. government, the flag, the Constitution and the military.[42]

Enforcing these laws were hardliners like A. Mitchell Palmer at the Justice Department. Palmer's like-minded protégé, J. Edgar Hoover, was equally zealous in enforcing the new law. As the head of the Division's Alien Enemy Bureau, Hoover collated a list of 1,400 suspicious Germans living in the United States. The bureau arrested 98 and designated 1,172 as arrestable.[43] Palmer and Hoover also took advantage of this new authority to take down Socialist and Anarchist groups in the United States. In September 1917, agents of the Bureau of Investigation, in conjunction with local law enforcement, raided every office of the International Workers of the World (IWW) across the United States within the space of twenty-four hours. The IWW was led by Big Bill Haywood and other Socialist leaders who were vocal about ending capitalism. In 1921, Big Bill Haywood, while out of jail on bail, fled to the Soviet Union and became an advisor to Vladimir Lenin in the Soviet Union. Alongside Americans John Reed and Charles Ruthenberg, Haywood was buried within the Kremlin walls after his death in 1928.[44]

After the Armistice was signed in November 1918, President Wilson appointed future president Herbert Hoover to head the European Relief and Rehabilitation Administration. Hoover was able to channel thirty-four million tons of American food, clothing and supplies to war-torn Europe.[45] Based on his results in preventing starvation in Europe during the First World War, Herbert Hoover would also provide famine relief to the Soviet Union in 1921. Responding to a plea for help from the Soviet government, the American Relief Administration (ARA) agreed to provide famine relief in the stricken areas.[46]

President Wilson proposed two major developments for lasting peace initiatives: Fourteen Points and the League of Nations. The Fourteen Points were a proposal made in a speech before Congress on January 8, 1918, outlining his vision for ending the First World War in a way that would prevent such a conflagration from occurring again. These points also were intended to keep Russia fighting on the Allied side, to boost Allied morale and to undermine the Central Powers.[47]

The League of Nations emanated from the Fourteen Points speech. Wilson called for a "general association of nations…formed under specific covenants for the purpose of affording mutual guarantees of political independence and territorial integrity to great and small states alike." The League of Nations initially failed for a variety of reasons, but the body acted as a precursor to what would become the United Nations.[48]

ALLIED INTERVENTION INTO RUSSIA

The world was shocked to its core when the Bolsheviks, led by Vladimir Lenin, Joseph Stalin, Leon Trotsky and others, ousted the Russian provisional government led by Alexander Kerensky in 1917. When the Bolsheviks made good on their promise to withdraw from the war with a separate peace with Germany, the Allies panicked due to the loss of the eastern front in Russia.

Great Britain asked Woodrow Wilson for United States assistance to take part in an intervention into Russia. Winston Churchill, known to most as a future prime minister of Great Britain during the Second World War, was one of the first to foresee the danger and damage that Communism was capable of inflicting on the world. As a minister of munitions, later secretary of state for war, Churchill in 1919 was noticeably clear when stating that Bolshevism should be "strangled in its cradle." Despite criticism by some advisors, Wilson acquiesced and supported sending five thousand troops into North Russia, landing in the port cities of Archangel and Murmansk on the White Sea. He also agreed to place an additional eight thousand troops in Vladivostok, Siberia. The American soldiers in North Russia and Siberia were placed under command of the British. This undesirable action in the ranks was not lost on these troops, whose ancestors fought the Revolutionary War and the War of 1812 against Great Britain.

The Allied intervention on all fronts threw most of their support behind the White Armies battling for control with the Bolshevik forces over the fate of Russia during the Russian Civil War. Archangel and Murmansk are two of only a few Russian port cities accessible by ship on the coast of the Arctic Circle in North Russia. These Americans joined forces with not only British commands but also Canadian, French, Polish and other nationalities fighting a hastily created Red Army. Being but two hundred miles away from Moscow, Leon Trotsky conscripted troops along the railways to fight these "imperialists."

Most of the Americans found themselves fighting along railways, rivers and other corridors that the Bolsheviks challenged. American soldiers were issued Russian rifles upon arrival. The guns jammed often and were inaccurate against an enemy they knew little about in a foreign place. Bad weapons, sickness, cold, frigid weather and a population that did not support the interventionists made for a bizarre episode in a strange, alien place.

On a separate front, several time zones from the North Russian Arctic forces, some eight thousand troops deployed to Vladivostok in Siberia on the Pacific coast. These men also joined a diverse group of interventionists from many countries. For a variety of reasons, including self-interest, tens of thousands of Japanese, French, British Commonwealth, Chinese and other forces intervened to fight on the battleground of far eastern Siberia. American troops took up defensive positions in that region, operating the Trans-Siberian Railroad and guarding rail lines in the Pacific coast in that country. "Wild" Bill Donovan, head of the wartime OSS during the Second World War, had his first intelligence assignment as part of the Expeditionary forces in Siberia. (See chapter 7 for more information.)

As the Treaty of Versailles was being signed in 1918, American soldiers were still stuck in Russia fighting. Many wives, mothers, sons and daughters wrote to President Wilson and other politicians asking why they were there. There was never acknowledgement received as to their purpose in Russia. Troops were finally sent home in 1919 from North Russia, and most troops were out of Siberia by 1920. While on the voyage home, those who had been in North Russia called themselves Polar Bears and wore a patch signifying such. After the withdrawal, the Bolsheviks declared victory over the White Russians and started a path of unifying the country that would become the Union of Soviet Socialist Republics in 1922. The Soviets would never forget the American intervention and used the event as ongoing propaganda against imperialists and capitalists around the world.[49]

President Wilson suffered a stroke in October 1919, just a year after the Versailles Treaty was signed. He had little success having the United States ratify the treaty, instead eventually negotiating its own peace with Germany. Wilson also did not see his idea of the League of Nations joined by the United States. Not seeking reelection in 1920, Wilson retired to Washington, D.C. Woodrow Wilson died in February 1924, within two weeks of Vladimir Lenin's death in the Soviet Union. Both suffered from strokes that neither could fully recover from.

6

ATOMS FOR PEACE

ATOMIC ENERGY FOR MANKIND

When the nuclear age began abruptly during the Second World War, there was a great deal of interest in applying this new energy to military purposes. Efforts to apply nuclear power to propulsion by both the United States and USSR resulted in the first icebreaker launched by the Soviet Union, in 1959, and the USS *Enterprise* aircraft carrier, launched in 1961 by the United States. The first nuclear submarine, USS *Nautilus*, was commissioned by the U.S. Navy in 1954, and the Navy continues to operate an entire fleet of nuclear submarines to this day. But merchant ships took a different approach, and the United States embarked on the creation of a peaceful ship called Nuclear Ship (NS) *Savannah*.

President Eisenhower's Atoms for Peace speech reflected his deep concern about "Atoms for War." The escalating nuclear arms race between the United States and the Soviet Union, which included the development of thermonuclear bombs, brought President Eisenhower to the United Nations. Since Hiroshima, the destructive power of nuclear weapons has increased dramatically. Nuclear weapons technology entered the arsenals of the Soviet Union, aided through espionage but born of the USSR's own nuclear program of technological development in 1949. President Eisenhower felt a moral imperative to warn the American people and the world of this new reality.[50]

In his speech to the United Nations, President Eisenhower pledged the United States to a leadership role in finding peaceful means to create and use atomic energy among nations to advance the cause of mankind.

The United States would be more than willing—it would be proud to take up with others "principally involved" the development of plans whereby such peaceful use of atomic energy would be expedited. Of those "principally involved" the Soviet Union must, of course, be one.

I would be prepared to submit to the Congress of the United States, and with every expectation of approval, any such plan that would, first, encourage world-wide investigation into the most effective peacetime uses of fissionable material, and with the certainty that the investigators had all the material needed for the conducting of all experiments that were appropriate; second, begin to diminish the potential destructive power of the world's atomic stockpiles; third, allow all peoples of all nations to see that, in this enlightened age, the great Powers of the Earth, both of the East and of the West, are interested in human aspirations first rather than in building up the armaments of war; fourth, open up a new channel for peaceful discussion and initiative at least a new approach to the many difficult problems that must be solved in both private and public conversations if the world is to shake off the inertia imposed by fear and is to make positive progress towards peace.

Against the dark background of the atomic bomb, the United States does not wish merely to present strength, but also the desire and the hope for peace. The coming months will be fraught with fateful decisions. In this Assembly, in the capitals and military headquarters of the world, in the hearts of men everywhere, be they governed or governors, may they be the decisions which will lead this world out of fear and into peace.

To the making of these fateful decisions, the United States pledges before you, and therefore before the world, its determination to help solve the fearful atomic dilemma—to devote its entire heart and mind to finding the way by which the miraculous inventiveness of man shall not be dedicated to his death but consecrated to his life.[51]

NUCLEAR SHIP *SAVANNAH*

NS *Savannah* is significant as the world's first application of nuclear power to a commercial ship and as the structure most associated with President Eisenhower's Atoms for Peace initiative. The combination passenger and cargo ship demonstrated to the world the safe and reliable operation of this new technology, which resulted in the establishing of a nuclear ship training program for civilian crew members, established procedures for commercial nuclear ships to enter domestic and foreign ports and identified a series of

Nuclear ship *Savannah* in port, San Francisco, California. *Internet Creative Commons.*

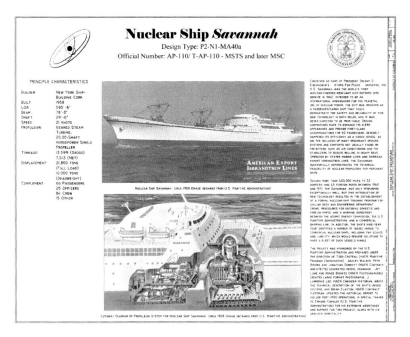

Design information and personal characteristics of nuclear ship *Savannah*. *Library of Congress.*

Forward superstructure, nuclear ship *Savannah*. *Library of Congress*.

issues that would require resolution in a second generation of commercial nuclear ships (disputes over crew pay scales, liability and commercial viability). In addition to its significant role in maritime history, *Savannah* served a unique public relations role as a floating exhibit on the peaceful use of nuclear energy.[52]

NS *Savannah* was constructed as a joint project of the former Atomic Energy Commission (AEC) and the Maritime Administration. It operated from 1962 to 1965 in experimental service, at which time the AEC issued *Savannah* commercial operating license number NS-1. *Savannah* continued in demonstration service as a cargo ship until 1970, when its active career ended. It was defueled in 1971, and the reactor became permanently inoperable in 1975–76. About 95 percent of the power plant is intact and remains on board the ship. *Savannah* is still licensed by the Nuclear Regulatory Commission (NRC is the successor to the AEC) and will remain so until nuclear decommissioning.

The defueling, active cleanup work and natural decay over thirty years has left only insignificant amounts of radioactive material aboard ship. This material is located in only a few well-monitored locations aboard ship.

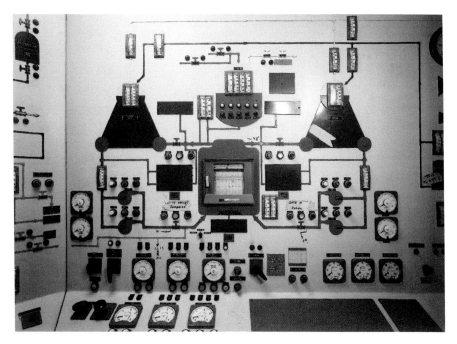

Detail of reactor and primary cooling system portion of control console's central panel, nuclear ship *Savannah*. *Library of Congress*.

Savannah was nominated to the National Register of Historic Places in 1981. It was named a Mechanical Engineering Landmark by the American Society of Mechanical Engineers in 1983. It was named a Nuclear Engineering Landmark by the American Nuclear Society in 1991 and finally declared a National Historic Landmark by the U.S. National Park Service on July 17, 1991.

The NS *Savannah* is presently located in the Port of Baltimore, Maryland, under a long-term lay berth contract with Canton Marine Terminals. The U.S. Maritime Administration Savannah Technical Staff of the Office of Ship Disposal manages the activities on board the ship, with strong emphasis on licensed facility operations and pre-decommissioning planning. The Maritime Administration intends to maintain *Savannah* in protective storage for some years into the future; however, under current law and regulation, the decommissioning process must be completed and *Savannah*'s operating license terminated no later than December 2031. In the normal course of NRC regulation, decommissioning would include the complete dismantling of the reactor. The historic ship community would like to see an exception made to allow for cleaning and then preservation of *Savannah*'s historic nuclear reactor aboard ship.[53] In total, only four nuclear-powered cargo vessels were ever built: NS *Savannah*, NS *Otto Hahn* in West Germany, the Russian container ship *Sevmorput* and the Japanese NS *Mutsu*.[54]

FORD MOTOR COMPANY FUND

Two years after the Atoms for Peace speech, President Dwight D. Eisenhower called for an international effort to apply nuclear science to peaceful purposes and expressed his hope that "private business and professional men throughout the world will take an interest and provide an incentive in finding new ways that this new science can be used...for the benefit of mankind and not destruction." In response, Henry Ford II, Benson Ford and Henry Clay Ford proposed that the Ford Motor Company Fund authorize an appropriation of $1 million to be granted at a rate of $100,000 annually for ten years to recognize outstanding contributions to the peaceful application of nuclear energy. The Atoms for Peace Awards, A Memorial to Henry Ford and Edsel Ford, was established by the directors of the fund to receive and administer the monies. The creation of the award was announced at the World Conference on the Peaceful Uses of Atomic Energy in Geneva, Switzerland, on August 8, 1955, by Admiral Lewis L. Strauss, chairman of the United States Atomic Energy Commission. A total of ten years of prizes were awarded, including to Dwight Eisenhower himself in 1969. Winners Niels Henrik David Bohr and Leo Szilard were famous physicists. Some years had multiple recipients who shared the prize.[55]

President Eisenhower's Atoms for Peace speech spurred other commitments that led to further advancement for not only military applications but also science and medical research and treatment. As nuclear energy fueled a fleet of U.S. submarines and generated electricity at more than one hundred power plants across the country, many of the world's hospitals, clinics and physicians today use therapies and diagnostic tools, such as magnetic resonance imaging (MRI) and positron emission topography (PET) scans, made possible by nuclear science. These and other breakthroughs in nuclear energy and medicine have fulfilled many of the peacetime promises of the Atomic Age. Medicine gained unexpected benefits from wartime research. In the early 1950s, the Atomic Energy Commission funded the Argonne Cancer Research Hospital in Chicago, which successfully pioneered the use of radiation in cancer treatment. Later called the Franklin McLean Memorial Research Institute, the hospital also developed radiology to diagnose and treat other diseases. On December 20, 1951, in a remote lab in Idaho, federal scientists produced the world's first nuclear-generated electricity. Scientists at Chicago's Argonne National Laboratory provided the fuel core needed to sustain the reaction, which lit up four light bulbs that frosty winter day.[56]

The Argonne National Laboratory was also helping to design the reactor for the world's first nuclear-powered submarine, USS *Nautilus*, which steamed for more than 513,550 nautical miles (951,090 kilometers). The next nuclear reactor model was Experimental Boiling Water Reactor, the forerunner of many modern nuclear plants, and Experimental Breeder Reactor II (EBR-II), which was sodium-cooled and included a fuel recycling facility. EBR-II was later modified to test other reactor designs, including a fast-neutron reactor and, in 1982, the Integral Fast Reactor concept—a revolutionary design that reprocessed its own fuel, reduced its atomic waste and withstood safety tests of the same failures that triggered the Chernobyl and Three Mile Island disasters.[57]

GOOD INTENTIONS, UNINTENDED FUTURE CONSEQUENCES

Iran became an example of how promoting peaceful nuclear power could become a liability in later years after an ally turned sour after the Iranian Revolution in 1979. As Iran was a participant in the program, Atoms for Peace laid the foundation for the country's nuclear program beginning in 1957. Eisenhower proposed that "governments principally involved, to the extent permitted by elementary prudence, should begin now and continue to make joint contributions from their stockpiles of normal uranium and fissionable material to an international atomic energy agency." The United States provided research reactors, fuel and scientific training to developing countries wanting civilian nuclear programs. In exchange, recipient states committed to using the technology and education for peaceful, civilian purposes only.

Iran's nuclear program began under Mohammad Reza Shah's rule in 1957, after the United States and Iran agreed to a civilian nuclear cooperation arrangement, known as the Cooperation Concerning Civil

Uses of Atoms, through the Atoms for Peace program. Two years later, the shah established the Tehran Nuclear Research Center (TNRC), located at the University of Tehran, and began to negotiate with the United States to provide Iran with nuclear technology and materials.

To meet these rising demands for nuclear engineers to research and build these programs, the Atomic Energy Organization of Iran concluded an agreement with the Massachusetts Institute of Technology (MIT) in 1975 to offer a specialized master's program that provided the Iranians with scientific and technological training on nuclear energy. This program provided Iran with its first set of professional nuclear engineers. Following the 1979 Iranian Revolution, the United States abruptly ended its civilian nuclear cooperation agreement with Iran and ended its supply of highly enriched uranium.[58]

The belief that atomic radiation might create super plants now seems counterintuitive. It is difficult to trace to a single source but may have arisen through reports from 1947, in which plants grown in the "atom-blasted" soil at Nagasaki were recorded as being double in size, and reportedly the "crop yield today from land at blast center is twice that from normal soil."[59]

The gamma gardens were research gardens, where a radiation source of Cobalt-60 was hoisted on a tower at the center of a circular field. Plants in the field would be exposed to varying degrees of radiation and accumulate mutations in their DNA. The radiation source was then lowered into a bunker, and researchers examined the plants, seeking favorable mutations. These were further developed until useful variants were produced. This process is still used in many areas, as the equipment is easier to set up and less expensive than equivalent gene-modification equipment.

Perhaps more interesting is the do-it-yourself aspect of atomic gardening that had a brief popularity. The Atoms for Peace effort also permitted citizens to get radioactive sources. One such citizen was an oral surgeon from Tennessee named C.J. Speas who irradiated seeds in his backyard and then sold them to home gardeners or to kids for science projects. He also attended home-and-garden shows and encouraged people to try their own atomic gardening. Radiation plant breeding has been largely supplanted by gene editing.[60]

Ideally, some plants might develop mutations that could prove beneficial and then be bred into normal plants. A peppermint plant resistant to particular strains of wilt, for example, was bred using atomic gardening.

Irradiated seeds became the "in" seeds for farmers, and "Atomic Energized" seeds were even marketed to housewives to conduct their own atomic gardening experiments at home. Ruby-red grapefruit, rice, wheat, pears, cotton, peas, sunflowers, bananas and countless other produce owe their present-day hardiness to the genetic modification afforded by atomic gardening.[61]

Although the experiments are mostly forgotten today, many crops and ornamental plant varieties still in common use descend from these tests that hoped to advance humanity by using "atoms for peace." These include the bright red Star Ruby grapefruit that comes with enhanced levels of the nutrient lycopene; Todd's Mitcham peppermint, which accounts for most of the world's production of menthol and mint oil; and probably almost every "super sweet" sweetcorn variety you have ever eaten. Ornamentals also attracted the mutation breeder's eye, with the practice widely used to create new orchid, pelargonium, rose, canna, streptocarpus and carnation varieties.[62]

THE PLOWSHARE PROGRAM

The Atomic Energy Commission established the Plowshare Program in June 1957 as another way to explore the peaceful uses of nuclear energy. The program took its name from the Bible (Isaiah 2:4), "They will beat their swords into plowshares." The purpose of the AEC program, instituted by the Lawrence Livermore National Laboratory, was to develop the technology necessary to use nuclear explosions for civil and industrial projects, such as the creation of harbors and canals and the stimulation of natural gas reservoirs. In 1967, the first of three joint government-industry experiments was conducted to investigate the feasibility of using nuclear explosions to stimulate natural gas production. Project Plowshare was terminated in 1977.[63]

7

CREATION OF THE
CENTRAL INTELLIGENCE AGENCY

One of the principal features of war under any circumstance is information and the need to know what the "other side" is doing. Of course, the world of espionage is nothing new, and the price for being caught is as much a reality as reaping the rewards of a dangerous game. General George Washington turned to Nathan Hale to spy during the American Revolutionary War against the British. Hale paid the ultimate price for his actions with his life. During the American Civil War, stories abound of women infiltrating both Union and Confederate sides of the conflict as caretakers and cooks. Women famously hid papers, swords, pistols and other war materiel in their hoopskirts. Mata Hari, the famous singer and dancer, was convicted of being a German spy during the First World War and executed by firing squad by the French in 1917.

The age of the Cold War brought about unique methods of spying in addition to old-fashioned information networks built on people who are the eyes and ears on the ground. Wiretaps were common, as were bugging phones and rooms with eavesdropping equipment. Eventually, spy planes and satellite intelligence that could read the license plate of a car from outer space became more than just science fiction.

The first known written account of espionage (and even a safe house) is, not surprisingly, of biblical origins. Allen Dulles, CIA director from 1953 to 1961, was said to have a plaque written on the world's second-oldest profession. The reader is left to understand the oldest profession. The first written account of spies is found in the Bible, giving credence to the idea

CIA Building in Langley, Virginia. *Library of Congress.*

spies were created by God. For those who fell asleep during Bible study, here are passages found in the Old Testament.[64]

> *Moses Sends Out 12 Spies*
> *The Lord said to Moses, [2] "Send men to explore Canaan, which I am giving to the Israelites. Send one leader from each of their ancestors' tribes."*
> *[3] So at the Lord's command, Moses sent these men from the Desert of Paran. All of them were leaders of the Israelites...*
> *[17] When Moses sent them to explore Canaan, he told them, "Go through the Negev and then into the mountain region. [18] See what the land is like and whether the people living there are strong or weak, few or many. [19] Is the land they live in good or bad? Do their cities have walls around them or not? [20] Is the soil rich or poor? Does the land have trees or not? Do your best to bring back some fruit from the land."*

After forty days, these men returned and reported their findings, making this the oldest reported spy mission in the world and on record as the world's second-oldest profession. And as we can see from this Bible lesson, the occupation of a spy was a creation from God—perhaps the only occupation created by God.

Rahab and the Spies
Then Joshua, son of Nun, secretly sent two spies from Shittim. "Go, look over the land," he said, "especially Jericho." So, they went and entered the house of a prostitute named Rahab and stayed there.
² The king of Jericho was told, "Look, some of the Israelites have come here tonight to spy out the land." ³ So the king of Jericho sent this message to Rahab: "Bring out the men who came to you and entered your house, because they have come to spy out the whole land."
⁴ But the woman had taken the two men and hidden them. She said, "Yes, the men came to me, but I did not know where they had come from. ⁵ At dusk, when it was time to close the city gate, they left. I do not know which way they went. Go after them quickly. You may catch up with them."

ESPIONAGE AS A WEAPON OF THE COLD WAR

The most effective means to wage war in the Cold War was espionage. In 1949, Americans and Western countries cringed as the Soviet Union tested its first nuclear bomb. A Soviet agent, Klaus Fuchs, and accompanying spy ring embedded in the Manhattan Project had enhanced the USSR's knowledge, allowing them to build an atomic bomb faster. Suspected of espionage, Fuchs managed to stay on in other atomic science capacity projects until 1949, when he was unmasked. In early 1950, Klaus Fuchs confessed to being a Soviet spy. That same year also bore witness to Communist Mao Tse Tung and his forces marching into Peking (now Beijing) and driving the Nationalist forces off the continent to the island of Formosa (now Taiwan). The Cold War was spreading quickly around the globe.

The second Red Scare was also well underway in 1948, as the House Un-American Activities Committee was ferreting out Communists and fellow travelers deeply entrenched in the government. Richard Nixon, then a congressman from California, was awash in testimony from such figures as Alger Hiss and Whittaker Chambers linking Hiss's influence as a Soviet collaborator to the fall of China. In a precursor to Joseph McCarthy's own allegations and investigations in the 1950s, those accused of Communism or Communist sympathies were surrounded by friends and professional acquaintances vouching for their innocence. Anti-Communist hearings and accusations were condemned, of which many were directed at those who worked in the higher levels of government. Many of these allegations were validated when the Venona Decrypts were finally declassified in 1995. Venona proved that Hiss, like many others, such as Harry Dexter White, Harry Hopkins and other New Deal progressives, had indeed some connection to the KGB or Soviet espionage.

It was in this environment, where threats were materializing, that a "need to know" what the other side was doing became a critical imperative.

CENTRALIZING INTELLIGENCE GATHERING

Intelligence gathering was piecemeal at best throughout other times in American history, and it wasn't until the Second World War that our country's foreign intelligence activities were coordinated government-wide. Before the war, the Department of State, the Federal Bureau of Investigation (FBI) and the United States Armed Services were collecting intelligence with no direction or coordination. President Franklin D. Roosevelt made a decision to create the Office of the Coordinator of Information (COI). Led by World War I hero General William "Wild Bill" Donovan, COI's main goal was to gather foreign intelligence related to the war.

Wild Bill's nickname came during his heroic actions during the First World War, where he earned two Purple Hearts, a Distinguished Service Medal plus a bronze oak leaf cluster, French Croix de Guerre and the Medal of Honor, the highest award in the U.S. military.[65]

General Donovan also had the distinction of beginning his intelligence career while serving with the American Expeditionary Force during the Russian Civil War in Siberia. It was in this theater that the origins of the Cold War and American distrust of the Soviets were sown. The Allied intervention into Russia, spearheaded by Winston Churchill and involving Woodrow Wilson's decision to intervene, was subsequently used to prop up the Soviet view of imperialists and capitalists. (See chapter 5 on Woodrow Wilson's presidency for more information.)[66]

As World War II progressed, Donovan and President Roosevelt reevaluated COI's size, organization and mission. At Donovan's suggestion, President Roosevelt transformed COI into a new office with a title that reflected the importance of strategy in intelligence gathering and clandestine operations.

Statue of William Donavan, 1980–2006. *Library of Congress.*

Often referred to as the agency's forerunner, the Office of Strategic Services (OSS) became the first centralized intelligence agency in American history. Staffed with a large number of women due to the needs of the war effort around the globe, then Colonel Bill Donovan led the OSS to collect and analyze strategic information and conduct unconventional and paramilitary operations. Though the new office met some resistance from other U.S. agencies, OSS continued to grow its worldwide intelligence capabilities through military, diplomatic and nonofficial cover. At its peak, OSS employed over thirteen thousand military personnel and civilians—35 percent of whom were women. OSS existed for just over three years, but in this time, it made a lasting contribution to our country, the world and the future of American intelligence.

CHANGING INTELLIGENCE ORGANIZATION AFTER THE WAR

At the conclusion of the Second World War, President Harry S. Truman abolished OSS along with many other war agencies. On President Truman's order, branches of OSS merged into a new office, the Strategic Services Unit (SSU). This organization was meant to be temporary and merged into the Central Intelligence Group (CIG).[67]

Unlike previous organizations of its kind, CIG was granted the authority to conduct independent research and analysis. This meant CIG could move beyond simply *coordinating* intelligence to *producing* intelligence. However, constrained by the Department of State and the Armed Services, President Truman soon recognized the need for a new, fully functional postwar intelligence organization.

In 1947, President Truman signed the National Security Act, establishing the Central Intelligence Agency (CIA) within the executive branch. The act charged the CIA with coordinating the nation's intelligence activities and, among other duties, collecting, evaluating and disseminating intelligence affecting national security. Approximately a third of this new agency comprised veterans of the OSS. In 1949, President Truman signed the Central Intelligence Agency Act. This legislation allowed the CIA to secretly fund intelligence operations and develop personnel procedures outside standard U.S. government practices.

By 1953, the agency was an established element of the U.S. government. Its contributions in the areas of political action and paramilitary warfare were recognized and respected. The CIA had grown six times in these six years and set up three of the five directorates we have today, which are

Directorate of Analysis
Directorate of Operations
Directorate of Science and Technology
Directorate of Digital Innovation
Directorate of Support[68]

These five core mission threads have characterized the agency's mission: clandestine collection, all-source analysis, covert action, partnerships and counterintelligence.

Until 1960, when a CIA U-2 plane piloted by Francis Gary Powers over the Soviet Union was shot down, very few people knew of the National Security Council or the Central Intelligence Agency. (See chapter 11 for further information.) It was an embarrassment to President Dwight Eisenhower, an otherwise stately war hero with the admiration of the public. Thereafter, public trust would wane in later years as questions and resistance emerged from the Kennedy assassination and the Vietnam War protests of the 1960s and 1970s. Knowledge of the excesses of the FBI through COINTELPRO would also hinder trust in the government.

In 1961, CIA employees moved from offices in Washington, D.C., to a new headquarters in Langley, Virginia. The original headquarters building was the first home designed specifically for agency officers and is still in use today.

COLD WAR AIR WAVES

One of the first actions of the newly created Central Intelligence Agency was propaganda aimed at the occupied countries of Eastern and Central Europe, in addition to the Soviet Union itself. Radio Free Europe (RFE) was created and grew in its early years through the efforts of the National Committee for a Free Europe (NCFE), an anti-Communist CIA front organization. Radio Liberty (RL) was separately founded in 1951 as the American Committee for Freedom for the Peoples of the USSR Inc.[69]

In order to reach populations effectively, these stations broadcasted in native languages to such countries as Bulgaria, Czechoslovakia, Hungary, Poland and Romania from within West Germany. Two years after its founding, Radio Liberty began broadcasting on March 1, 1953. Four days later, Soviet dictator Joseph Stalin died. In a unique happenstance with U.S. Air Force eavesdroppers in West Berlin, it was purported that one Airman Johnny Cash, the future singer, who was on duty at the time, became one of the first Americans to learn of Stalin's death.

While Radio Free Europe and Radio Liberty received funds covertly from the CIA, they also drew widespread public support from Eisenhower's "Crusade for Freedom" campaign. Begun in 1950, Crusade for Freedom had attracted private money from the American people and also proffered a gift of a Freedom Bell to the people of West Berlin later that year. Custodianship of the Freedom Bell was accepted by Mayor Ernst Reuter on October 24, 1950, who declared, in part: "The sound of this bell will not only be heard in Berlin and throughout Germany; It will ring not only over the ocean to the great American people; it will also clearly be heard in the East. We know that the peoples of Warsaw, Prague, Budapest, and Sofia are longing to listen to this sound of hope. Moreover, we are sure that even the Russian people would be in accord with us if they could freely express their will."[70]

The CIA still funded a sizable $5 million to the operation costs of the Crusade for Freedom, and citizens of the Soviet Union and Communist Bloc countries could secretly listen to airwaves from Germany. Of corollary interest to these propaganda programs was the recruitment of ex-Nazis in Germany to undercut the Soviet menace in Europe, who assisted in maintaining Radio Liberty's programming and building operations.[71]

The Soviet Union took steps to jam radio signals and had enormous success in doing such in major metropolitan areas. However, citizens in the Communist sphere both in Russia and the Iron Curtain countries would simply take their shortwave radios outside of city limits and pick up broadcasts elsewhere. Jamming began to cease during the era of Glasnost in 1988 under Mikhail Gorbachev.[72]

OPERATION MOCKINGBIRD

In 1973, the CIA's broadcasting expertise, whose aim was neutralizing international Communism abroad, was allegedly turned toward domestic mass media and American citizens. The U.S. Senate Watergate Committee accused the CIA of domestic surveillance abuses directed by the U.S. government. In 1976, the Church Committee, convening as the Senate Select Committee to Study Governmental Operations with Respect to Intelligence Activities, published a report (*Intelligence Activities and the Rights of Americans*). These allegations confirmed earlier stories charging that the CIA had cultivated relationships with private institutions, including the press, and stated that it found fifty journalists who had official, but secret, relationships with the CIA. Since no names were ever revealed, there was widespread speculation that many newspapers, such as the *Washington Post*, were allegedly aligned with the CIA and domestic surveillance.[73]

OPERATION ROLLBACK AND
THE VOLUNTEER FREEDOM CORPS

With refugees fleeing en masse from war-torn Europe, camps were set up around the continent to receive them. As these refugees awaited settlement in other countries, some individuals were sought out by the Central

Intelligence Agency to undertake the mission of overthrowing Soviet-influenced and occupied countries. This was an opportunity for the United States clandestine apparatus to not just contain Communism but become proactive.

George Georgiev (later Georgieff after moving to the United States) was one such individual. Born in 1930 in the village of Dinevo, Bulgaria, George Georgiev grew up during the years of the Second World War, witnessing the Bulgarian Communist coup in 1944 that was a precursor to decades of Communist rule and Soviet influence. George, along with many other young men of his age, was involved with the opposition movement and refused to join the Communist Party. Because of these actions and beliefs, George and others like him were not allowed to attend college. After a friend reported his opposition activities to the local party leaders in April 1950, nineteen-year-old George and another friend left their families and homes to escape Bulgaria and avoid being put in a labor camp, as his cousin and other acquaintances had been. The group walked for three days to Greece and crossed the border on foot. They were eventually picked up by Greek soldiers, processed as refugees and taken to a refugee camp near Athens.

George had lived in the refugee camp for a few months when representatives from the CIA came to the camp to recruit men to train for espionage work. Although George had been waiting for a transport to emigrate, he decided to stay and assist the CIA, since he hoped that it meant he would be able to return to his homeland of Bulgaria. In January 1951, George and about twenty other young men from the refugee camp were flown to Germany to begin their training at a resort villa in the Alps. They trained for three months, learning Morse code and transmitting messages, as well as physical self-defense.

After training, George and the rest of his group were sent back to Greece. They were based there for five years, during which time George crossed the border back into Bulgaria to collect information about the Communist Party's activities. Groups of two or three men would cross the border and set up base for a few months. They hid in the mountains and made contact with locals, collecting information that they in turn coded and sent back to the base in Athens. It was dangerous work; one of George's friends was discovered by the militia and killed at the border.

In 1955, Greece and Bulgaria entered into a treaty, and the CIA was no longer allowed to operate in Greece. As such, the men were relieved of their duties. By this time, one of George's uncles was in Germany, so George was able to emigrate to join him. He lived in Germany for two years, working for the American Army as a guard at military depots until he received his visa and a sponsorship to come to America in 1957. He landed in Richmond, Virginia, and soon joined some friends who had settled in Chicago, Illinois. There he worked as a welder and eventually a tool and die maker. In 1958, he married Ursula Mursewski, who had emigrated from East Germany. They raised two children and lived quietly in the midwestern United States until George passed away in 2012.[74]

Operation Rollback would be molded into other clandestine programs in later years. Project AEDEPOT was one such top-secret program begun in 1956 as a means to train small groups of foreign nationals behind the Iron Curtain countries for dispatch to designated foreign targets when hostilities were imminent.[75]

DEPOSING FIDEL CASTRO BY WAY OF THE MAFIA

Fidel Castro's revolutionary career began while he was enrolled at the School of Law of the University of Havana when he participated in resistance movements in the Dominican Republic and Colombia. He became active in Cuban politics after graduating in 1950, and he prepared to run for legislative office in the 1952 elections. Those elections were canceled when Fulgencio Batista forcibly seized power. Castro began organizing a resistance movement against Cuba's new dictator, leading several ill-fated attempts against Batista's forces, such as the assault on Santiago de Cuba and another on Cuba's eastern coast. The tide of battle would turn, however: Castro's guerrilla warfare campaign and his propaganda efforts succeeded in eroding the power of Batista's military and popular support while also attracting volunteers to the revolutionary cause. Batista was forced to flee the country in 1959. Shortly after, Castro assumed complete authority over Cuba's new government.

It is widely reputed, and was partially corroborated, by the Church Committee hearings that during the Kennedy administration, the Central Intelligence Agency recruited Salvatore "Sam" Giancana and other mobsters to assassinate Fidel Castro. Giancana reportedly said that the CIA and the Cosa Nostra were "different sides of the same coin." Documents released in 2017 showed the Giancana connection to the CIA and to private investigator Robert Maheu. Judith Exner claimed to be the mistress of both Giancana and JFK and that she delivered communications between them about Castro. Giancana's daughter Antoinette has stated that her father was performing a fraud to pocket millions of CIA dollars.[76]

Documents released in 1997 revealed that some Mafiosi worked with the CIA on assassination attempts against Castro. CIA documents released during 2007 confirmed that during the summer of 1960, CIA recruited ex-FBI agent Maheu to meet with the West Coast representative of the Chicago mob, Johnny Roselli. When Maheu contacted Roselli, Maheu hid that he was sent by the CIA, instead portraying himself as an advocate for international corporations. He offered $150,000 to have Castro killed, but Roselli refused any pay. Roselli introduced Maheu to two men he called Sam Gold and Joe. "Sam Gold" was Giancana; "Joe" was Santo Trafficante Jr., the Tampa/Miami syndicate boss and one of the most powerful mobsters in pre-revolution Cuba. Glenn Kessler of the *Washington Post* explained: "After Fidel Castro led a revolution that toppled the government of Fulgencio Batista in 1959, the CIA was desperate to eliminate Castro. So, the agency sought out a partner equally worried about Castro—the Mafia, which had lucrative investments in Cuban casinos."[77]

According to the declassified CIA "Family Jewels" documents, Giancana and Trafficante were contacted in September 1960 about the possibility of an assassination attempt by Maheu after Maheu had contacted Roselli, a Mafia member in Las Vegas and Giancana's number-two man. Maheu had presented himself as a representative of numerous international businesses in Cuba that Castro was expropriating. He offered $150,000 for the "removal" of Castro through this operation. (The documents suggest that Roselli, Giancana and Trafficante did not accept any payment for the job.) Giancana suggested using poison pills to dose Castro's food and drink. The CIA gave these pills to Giancana's nominee, Juan Orta, whom Giancana presented as a corrupt official in the new Cuban government and who had access to Castro. After six attempts to introduce the poison into Castro's food, Orta abruptly demanded to be relieved from the mission, giving the job to another, unnamed participant. Later, Giancana and Trafficante made a second attempt using Anthony Verona, the commander of the Cuban Exile Junta, who had, according to Trafficante, become "disaffected with the apparent ineffectual progress of the Junta." Verona requested $10,000 in expenses and $1,000 worth of communications equipment. How much work was performed for the second attempt is unknown, as the entire program was canceled soon thereafter due to the Bay of Pigs invasion in April 1961. The following year, the Cuban Missile Crisis became yet another Cold War flashpoint, this time with nuclear missiles being placed

Ernesto "Che" Guevara with Fidel Castro. *Internet Creative Commons.*

in Cuba by the Soviets. Nuclear war was barely averted, with missiles sent back by barge to the Soviet Union when Nikita Khrushchev blinked on the verge of disaster.

According to the "Family Jewels," Giancana asked Maheu to wire the room of his then mistress Phyllis McGuire, whom he suspected of having an affair with comedian Dan Rowan. Although documents suggest Maheu acquiesced, the device was not placed due to the arrest of the agent who had been tasked with planting it. According to the documents, Robert F. Kennedy prohibited the prosecution of the agent and of Maheu, who was soon linked to the wire attempt, at the CIA's request. Giancana and McGuire, who had a long-lasting affair, were originally introduced by Frank Sinatra. According to Antoinette Giancana, during part of the affair, McGuire had a concurrent affair with President Kennedy.[78]

CIA ROLE IN IRAN-CONTRA

The Iran-Contra affair was a seminal moment in Cold War history in the 1980s. The Sandinistas, a Marxist National Liberation Front, ousted the Somoza dynasty in Nicaragua. In his anti-Communist crusade, Ronald Reagan backed the Contras in Nicaragua, fighting against the pro-Marxist Sandinista government and adhering to the Monroe Doctrine. When Democrats in Congress blocked the funding of these "freedom fighters" under the Boland Amendment, the Reagan administration was forced to find other means to support the Contras. A plan was then hatched to sell arms (notably tube-fired anti-tank and anti-aircraft missiles) to Iran, in exchange for help securing the release of American hostages in the Middle East. Iran was embroiled in a war with its neighbor Iraq, led by Saddam Hussein, at that time. The proceeds of these arms sales were then funneled to assist the Contras in Nicaragua. There have also been rumors and evidence that the drug trade in Central and South America was intertwined in arming and training the Contras. This allegation has been noted in books and documentaries, including the stories of pilots Barry Seal and Gary Betzner, who personify supposed real-life cases of being involved in these efforts.[79]

A catalyst of public opinion in the United States about the war in Nicaragua was the case of Eugene Hasenfus, a former Marine during the Cold War. Hasenfus found himself at the center of the Iran-Contra Affair when a cargo plane carrying weapons intended for the Contras was shot down by the Sandinistas in Nicaragua on October 5, 1986. Hasenfus was the only survivor of the crash. Under duress, Hasenfus admitted being hired by the CIA to drop supplies to the Contras by air. He was tried and convicted in Nicaragua and, on November 15, 1986, sentenced to thirty years in prison for terrorism and other charges. He was released in December that year.[80]

CIA MUSEUM

The legacy of the CIA has been intertwined with the Cold War since its inception in 1947. In 1972, former CIA Executive Director William E. Colby had the idea for an agency museum filled with artifacts of historical significance to create "a very selective accumulation of truly unique items." Since the museum is located at Langley headquarters and not open to the public, virtual resources are available via the CIA website. Of these virtual exhibits, the CIA website states articles in its possession include a robotic bug that is actually a bug and a makeup compact that hides a secret message. The collection includes spy gadgets, specialized weaponry and espionage memorabilia that spans the pre–World War II origins through today.[81]

In addition to the CIA Museum, a Memorial Wall was created in July 1974 to honor former officers lost in the line of duty when 31 stars were chiseled into the marble wall just inside the building entrance in Langley. There was no dedication ceremony, no pictures taken and no fanfare. The stars and inscriptions simply appeared, and the stars sat in silent commemoration for the next thirteen years without ceremony. That changed in 1987, and every year since then, the agency has gathered to remember its fallen officers. More stars have since been added, and 140 stars exist as of this writing, with the names of thirty-seven officers remaining secret.[82] Of those officers who perished serving the United States during the Cold War era, some of the names of officers have been published. They include:[83]

DOUGLAS MACKIERNAN was the first CIA employee to be killed in the line of duty and the first star on the wall. As the People's Republic of China took control in 1949, State Department officials like Mackiernan were instructed to leave. Mackiernan was ordered to stay behind, however, to destroy cryptographic equipment and aid anti-Communist Nationalists. He was shot by Tibetan border guards while escaping the country in 1950.

STEPHEN KASARDA JR. died in 1960 while stationed in Southeast Asia. He was working with air supply missions being flown into Tibet. These missions were to support Tibet to continue as an autonomous region, aiding against direct conflict with the advance of the Chinese Communist government ideology and political persecution.

Four CIA Lockheed U-2 pilots who died in plane crashes: WILBURN S. ROSE (d. May 15, 1956), FRANK G. GRACE (d. August 31, 1956), HOWARD CAREY (d. September 17, 1956) and EUGENE "BUSTER" EDENS (d. April 1965). Rose, Grace, Carey and Edens were honored with stars in 1974.

JAMES J. MCGRATH died following an accident while working on a high-power German transmitter in January 1957.

TUCKER GOUGELMANN was a paramilitary operations officer from the CIA's Special Activities Division who worked in the CIA from 1949 to 1972, serving in Europe, Afghanistan, Korea and Vietnam. Gougelmann returned to Saigon in the spring of 1975 in an attempt to secure exit visas for loved ones after North Vietnam had launched a major offensive. He missed his final flight out of Saigon and was captured by the North Vietnamese, who tortured him for eleven months before he died.

KENNETH E. HAAS and ROBERT C. AMES died in the 1983 Beirut Embassy bombing that also killed 241 American military personnel. Their stars were placed on the wall in 2007. (See chapter 4 for more information.)

MATTHEW GANNON, CIA deputy chief of station in Beirut, Lebanon, was one of at least 4 American intelligence officers aboard the 1988 Pan Am Flight 103 killed in an explosion in flight over Lockerbie, Scotland. A memorial also exists in Arlington National Cemetery as the Lockerbie Memorial Cairn, dedicated to 190 Americans who were killed in the terrorist attack linked to the government of the late Muammar Gaddafi.[84]

8

THE FEDERAL BUREAU OF INVESTIGATION

FIGHTING ENEMIES WITHIN

T he mission of the Federal Bureau of Investigation (FBI) is simple: to protect the American people and uphold the Constitution of the United States.[85]

The FBI is an intelligence-driven and threat-focused national security organization with both intelligence and law enforcement responsibilities. It is the principal investigative arm of the U.S. Department of Justice and a

FBI Headquarters Building, Washington, D.C. *Library of Congress.*

full member of the U.S. Intelligence Community. The FBI has the authority and responsibility to investigate specific crimes assigned to it and to provide other law enforcement agencies with cooperative services, such as fingerprint identification, laboratory examinations and training. The FBI also gathers, shares and analyzes intelligence, both to support its own investigations and those of its partners and to better understand and combat the security threats facing the United States.[86]

Behind this straightforward mission and statement of purpose for the FBI is a foundation steeped in Cold War history and the makings of one of the most famous government leaders in American history: J. Edgar Hoover.

J. EDGAR HOOVER, THE COLD WAR AND FIGHTING COMMUNISM

Seeing Red: The First Red Scare of 1919–20

Most Americans learned and continue to use the catchall names of Joe McCarthy and McCarthyism as derogatory terms for hunting enemies in their midst and destroying reputations. Few would connect the first Red Scare with the events of the Bolshevik regime in Russia taking shape in 1918. An undertow of American sympathizers to the Soviet movement was gaining steam domestically, especially among labor unions, and creating civil unrest, as wartime laws, price controls and wages were being contested. These events were occurring as American troops returned from the Arctic Circle and Siberia fighting the Bolsheviks and the early Red Army during the Russian Civil War.

The American Legion was created by veterans of the First World War and chartered in 1919 as a patriotic veterans' service organization by Congress. The Red Menace created an extraordinary sense of anxiety among the public, and these members returning from war were eager to do their part in defending American idealism. Hence, the American Legion included in its charter the promise to "uphold and defend a 100% Americanism" in its preamble. To this day, the same preamble is spoken and referenced at every meeting and convention held by the American Legion in the United States.

On the home front, a young J. Edgar Hoover was making his mark against the Red Menace as well. Labor unrest was being fomented by Communists, Anarchists and Socialists. Bombs were being sent to various political figures, with deaths and dismemberment common in those violent incidents. As a result, a hard line against radicals and subversives in the United States was undertaken. Various suspects adhering to this un-American activity were targeted during the Red Scare in 1919. Raids were authorized by A. Mitchell Palmer, then Justice Department head. Hoover's efficiency drew the attention of Attorney General Palmer, who appointed him to lead the General Intelligence Division (GID), created to gather information on radical groups. In 1919, the GID conducted raids without search warrants and arrested hundreds of individuals from suspected radical groups.[87]

The question became what to do with these radicals who were deemed harmful to U.S. interests. Perhaps if these radicals loved Communism

Informal photo of J. Edgar Hoover, director of FBI, Department of Justice, April 5, 1940. *Library of Congress.*

so much, why not let them live in Communist Russia? J. Edgar Hoover determined that these individuals would become "Christmas presents" for Lenin and Trotsky. In December 1919, a ship commissioned as the USS *Buford* was utilized by the U.S. Navy to send these "presents" to Bolshevik Russia. Using intermediaries, some 249 souls from the United States were sent for a three-month voyage to Finland. (Since there was no diplomatic recognition of the new Bolshevik Russia, the members of the Soviet Ark were dropped off in Finland.) It was at the Finnish border to Russia where these radicals and self-identified Communists would walk into the Soviet Union. The Soviets, never shy about pomp and circumstance in these situations, greeted these "Christmas presents" with cheers and a big band reception playing the Russian national anthem. The 249 members of the Soviet Ark were hailed as heroes for upholding Communist beliefs.[88]

Director of the Bureau of Investigation

In 1924, A. Mitchell Palmer was forced out of the attorney general position. In his place, a young J. Edgar Hoover, all of twenty-nine years old, was appointed to the position of director of the Bureau of Investigation by President Calvin Coolidge.[89] After organizing the Bureau to his liking, and continuing as the director after the organization was renamed the Federal

Bureau of Investigation, Hoover set his sights on taking down gangsters such as Al Capone and John Dillinger. As the 1930s Great Depression lingered and with war on the horizon, Americans in larger numbers were drawn to other political philosophies. Nazism, Communism and the threat of Japanese spies on American soil were of real concern, and the FBI was assigned the task of surveillance. Likewise, since there was no agency dedicated to foreign intelligence, the FBI was also tasked by President Franklin Roosevelt to provide espionage in the Western Hemisphere, which was largely contained to South and Latin America. The latter regions were under suspicion, as they had attracted émigrés from Germany and conducted influence operations on policies.

The Venona Project

It was on September 1, 1947, that the FBI's liaison to the NSA, Special Agent S. Wesley Reynolds, was briefed by Colonel Carter Clarke on the breaks in Soviet diplomatic messages. Clarke asked Reynolds if the Bureau knew of any Soviet cover names that might help his team's effort. Reynolds soon turned over a list of two hundred known cover names that the FBI had acquired. Most of them had not been found in the encrypted traffic to that point.[90]

In 1948, connections to the Julius Rosenberg spy ring were taking shape by decrypting this Soviet traffic. At the same time, the House Un-American Activities Committee (HUAC) was moving forward in investigating Alger Hiss with Whittaker Chambers. HUAC also had utilized Elizabeth Bentley in ferreting out Communists in the federal government. She and others would testify in the hearings. Bentley was considered untrustworthy in some respects due to her alcoholism and overexaggeration. However, Bentley was indeed a Soviet courier connecting agents and Soviet handlers in New York City. She was able to identify twenty-seven employees as Soviet agents and a further twenty-one non-government agents with allegiance to the Soviet Union.

William Walter Remington was one such Soviet agent. Remington was a government economist accused by Elizabeth Bentley of cooperating in espionage for the Soviet Union during World War II. He was convicted of lying under oath in 1953 for denying that he had provided Bentley with technical data related to war production and earlier ties to a Communist group. Remington was murdered in jail in 1954.[91]

Angela Calomiris, photographer and FBI informant within the U.S. Communist Party. *Library of Congress.*

Further breakthroughs were ascertained with the Venona project. When the British were interested in a case involving an agent codenamed "REST," they inquired with the FBI. All of the evidence pointed to Klaus Fuchs. Fuchs had been embedded in the Manhattan Project and passed along secrets to Soviet agents in Great Britain. After Fuchs confessed to spying and passing along atomic secrets that sped up the Soviet atomic program, he also provided contacts and other associates in the spy ring. This in turn led to David Greenglass, whose sister was Ethel Rosenberg. In a further breakthrough, Ethel's husband, Julius Rosenberg, was identified as ANTENNA. The couple was convicted and then executed for espionage activities in 1953. Through Venona, the FBI identified 108 persons involved in Soviet espionage, 64 of whom had been unknown to the FBI prior to the project. The memo also showed that the FBI had greatly expanded the details about the Soviet networks broken with the help of Venona intelligence. The FBI now had a clear view of other Soviet intelligence operations in the United States too, including its efforts against Leon Trotsky and his followers, the White Russians and U.S. technical targets.[92]

Gene Grabeel and the Founding of Venona

With men off to war in vast numbers in 1942, the Venona Project was teeming with many women code breakers and cryptographers. Gene Grabeel of Lee County, Virginia, was a high school teacher when a friend suggested she work for the Signal Intelligence Service in 1942 in order to make more money. Women who were college graduates could work near Washington, D.C., with a starting salary of $1,800 a year plus Saturday bonuses, much more than a schoolteacher's salary. She accepted without knowing exactly what the job entailed, since it was deemed classified. After reporting to Arlington Hall, she encountered a profession that would become her career for thirty-six years.

The problem that Gene Grabeel was first asked to address, and Meredith Gardner eventually took on as the war ended and the importance of his work on German and Japanese codes subsided, was what to do with tens of thousands of encrypted Soviet telegrams intercepted between 1942 and early 1946. On February 1, 1943, she founded the Venona project, a counterintelligence program aimed at decrypting Soviet communications. After dedicating decades to breaking the Soviet codes, Grabeel retired from service in 1978. Venona would soon be phased out due to its age in 1980. She died at age ninety-four in 2015, in Blackstone, Virginia. After the 1995 declassification of the Venona project, Grabeel and others were recognized by the Central Intelligence Agency as American heroes.[93]

Venona Decryption Leaked to the Soviets

Jones Orin York, identified as Venona cover name NEEDLE, was an aircraft worker in California during the Second World War. In April 1950, he was questioned by the FBI and alleged that a former case officer of his was an Armed Forces Security Agency (AFSA) employee named William Weisband. AFSA suspended Weisband a month later. Weisband, an NKVD agent who was not a cryptographer but a Ukrainian who spoke fluent Russian, passed along this crucial information to the Soviets. Along with Kim Philby, first secretary to the British Embassy in Washington, D.C., the Venona program was then well known to the Soviets. Weisband served a year in jail for contempt for failing to appear in front of a grand jury and never worked in government again.[94]

COLD WAR MANHUNT: SOVIET COLONEL RUDOLF ABEL

One of the largest cases of espionage involved Soviet Colonel Rudolf Abel. Following the discovery of a hollow nickel, a tip given to a newsboy in 1953 in New York City, the FBI conducted a search for a Soviet spymaster. A series of breaks, through the interviewing of Soviet defectors and consequent leads, finally emerged in the case over the next few years. In 1957, the FBI raided the home of Rudolf Abel, a Soviet spy who had been working in the United States as a KGB spymaster since 1944. Once the FBI landed Abel, he was sentenced to prison and spared the death penalty. James Donovan, lawyer for Abel, had floated the idea to keep Abel alive and use him as a bargaining chip in a hypothetical swap for an American asset in the future. That day came when Abel was exchanged for Francis Gary Powers, a U-2 pilot shot down over the Soviet Union in 1960. The exchange was held over the Glienicke Bridge in Berlin in 1962 and depicted in the 2015 Steven Spielberg / Tom Hanks movie *Bridge of Spies*.

COINTELPRO

COINTELPRO (Counterintelligence Program) was a counterintelligence program the FBI ran from 1956 to 1971. During the Cold War, J. Edgar Hoover's staunch anti-Communism was welcomed by most Americans. Nevertheless, there were any number of unconstitutional actions by the Bureau alleged by its many unending critics. Efforts conducted by the U.S. Federal Bureau of Investigation were aimed at surveilling, infiltrating, discrediting and disrupting domestic American political organizations. Methods authorized included infiltration, burglaries, setting up illegal wiretaps, planting forged documents and spreading false rumors about key members of target organizations.[95]

Most American organizations targeted during this era were suspected to be influenced by foreign actors, notably Communist sympathizers and Soviet

FBI opens JFK assassination files. *Library of Congress.*

front groups that provided funding to such organizations. But surveillance did not stop with the Communist Party USA, Socialist Party, anti–Vietnam War groups or even white supremacist groups the FBI was tasked to monitor. Instead, it also vacuumed up the civil rights and feminist movements, Puerto Rico statehood, farm labor and American Indian movements and many others without purpose.[96]

One of the most egregious incidents involved sending an anonymous letter and tape recording to Martin Luther King Jr. in 1964. Allegedly, evidence of King's sexual indiscretions was delivered to King's address with a message stating, "King, there is only one thing left for you to do. You know what it is. You have just 34 days in which to do." The "34 days" coincided with Martin Luther King Jr.'s acceptance of the Nobel Peace Prize on December 10, 1964.

During the Church Committee hearings and investigations in 1975, a copy of the "suicide letter" was discovered in the work files of William C. Sullivan, deputy FBI director. He has been suggested as its author, even though underhanded tactics of the FBI of planting Sullivan as the fall guy would be an equally plausible possibility, since he and J. Edgar Hoover were not on good terms after Sullivan departed the FBI in 1971.

By the time Hoover entered service under his eighth president in 1969, the media, the public and Congress had grown suspicious that the FBI might be abusing its authority. Through the Church Committee, the public would be more informed of possible egregious behavior uncovered through investigations. For the first time in his bureaucratic career, Hoover endured widespread criticism, and Congress responded by passing laws requiring Senate confirmation of future FBI directors and limiting their tenure to ten years. On May 2, 1972, Hoover died at the age of seventy-seven. He was a controversial American icon who was effective at shaping anti-Communist policies, modernizing the FBI and its staffing and taking on gangsters and bootlegging. His legacy will continue to be reexamined as more information is declassified over time.

Of note is Mark Felt, who rose to deputy director after the death of J. Edger Hoover and later became the notorious Deep Throat, the source for the Watergate Investigations that would lead to President Richard Nixon's resignation in 1974. In 1980, Felt was convicted of having violated the civil rights of people thought to be associated with members of the Weather Underground by ordering FBI agents to break into their homes and search the premises as part of an attempt to prevent bombings. He was ordered to pay a fine but was pardoned by President Ronald Reagan during his appeal.

FBI ACADEMY QUANTICO

The FBI Academy found its way to Quantico, Virginia, in an interesting fashion. It began with the so-called Kansas City Massacre. In June 1933, three police officers and one Bureau agent escorting a prisoner through a Missouri train station were killed when "Pretty Boy" Floyd and other criminals opened fire on them. Following the public outcry, FBI agents were given the authority to make arrests and to carry weapons for the first time.

In order to learn marksmanship and take target practice, the FBI needed a safe, out-of-the-way place, finding one such place via the United States Marine Corps. Beginning in 1934, the Marine Corps allowed the FBI to start using the firing ranges on its base in Quantico, Virginia, about thirty-five miles southwest of the nation's capital, and they have coexisted there ever since.

Meanwhile, the Bureau was moving into the training business. In the early 1920s, the Bureau began formal training for agents, and the first organized agent school launched in 1929 in Washington, D.C. It included classroom training, practical exercises in fingerprinting and evidence collection and physical instruction on the rooftop of the Justice Department. By the late 1930s, the gun ranges used by the Marines were not meeting the more specialized law enforcement needs. The FBI needed a principal place to instruct and house all the police officers and special agents now training. The Marine Corps allowed the FBI to construct their own firing range and, in 1940, the first classroom building on the main section of the base. The FBI Academy was born.

In 1965, the Bureau received approval to build a brand-new complex at Quantico. Construction began in 1969, and a new home was on the horizon.

In line with the recommendations of a national commission on the need for more standardized police training, in 1935 the FBI launched a Police Training School, the forerunner of today's National Academy program. The high-level police professionals learned investigative and scientific techniques, studied management principles, did practical exercises and received firearms training at the gun range at Quantico. Many of the graduates opened training classes back home to share what they had learned.

On May 7, 1972, a mere five days after J. Edgar Hoover died, the new, expanded and modernized FBI Academy was opened. The complex included more than two dozen classrooms, eight conference rooms, twin seven-story dormitories, a one-thousand-seat auditorium, a dining hall, a full-sized gym and swimming pool, a fully equipped library and a new firing range—not to mention much-needed enhancements like specialized classrooms for forensic science training, four identification labs, more than a dozen darkrooms and a mock-city classroom and crime scene room for practical exercises. The ample facilities enabled National Academy classes to expand tenfold, to more than two hundred students per session, including more from overseas.[97]

9

INFAMOUS SOVIET MOLES ARRESTED BY THE FBI

Although there were many individuals in federal government employment arrested for espionage in conjunction with aiding the Soviet Union during and in the aftermath of the Cold War, limitations on the scope of this book mean that it cannot cover all cases. Thankfully, there are many more volumes providing depth to the many stories of Cold War history dedicated to the likes of Edward Lee Howard, Jonathan Pollard, Larry Wu-tai Chin and countless others who betrayed the United States for various reasons: money, debts, disillusionment or even frustration over lack of job mobility in the agencies.

Here follow a few notable cases in which these moles were eventually caught and jailed for their actions in providing the Soviet Union with damning information: Earl Edwin Pitts, John Walker Jr., Robert Hanssen and Aldrich Ames. These men not only abused their positions to harm the United States for personal motives and gain but also gave up valuable lives of Soviet agents.

EARL EDWIN PITTS

According to the FBI, on December 18, 1996, Earl Edwin Pitts, a thirteen-year veteran special agent of the FBI, was arrested for espionage at the FBI Academy in Quantico, Virginia. At the time of his arrest, Pitts was an instructor at the Academy. The FBI had reassigned Pitts from FBI Headquarters, where he had access to classified information, nearly sixteen months earlier, to the FBI training academy in Quantico. His access to classified information was much reduced in the process. The FBI Washington Field Office then put together a complex false flag operation that cost almost $1 million, culminating in the arrest of Pitts.[98]

During the investigation, which began in 1994, the FBI determined that Pitts conducted espionage from 1987 to 1992 for the KGB and its successor, Russia's SVR. Pitts shared classified information concerning FBI personnel, ongoing investigations, counterintelligence program strategies and operational methodology.

According to an FBI press release, from 1987 to the present, Pitts conspired with officers of the KGB and SVR to commit espionage. The conspiracy included numerous trips that Pitts made from Virginia to the New York area "in connection with his espionage activities," the affidavit said.[99] "Pitts remained an agent of the SVRR in a dormant capacity" from 1992 to the present. In the 1987 to 1992 period, the affidavit noted, "Pitts received from the KGB and SVRR in excess of $224,000."

According to the affidavit, in 1987 an official at the Soviet Mission to the United Nations in New York City, identified only as a "cooperating witness" or CW, received a letter containing surveillance information about the CW's activities and requesting a meeting with him, if he were a KGB officer, or with an actual KGB officer.

Pitts graduated from the FBI Academy as a new agent in 1983 and was assigned to the former Alexandria, Virginia Field Office (now part of the Washington Field Office) and later to the Fredericksburg, Virginia Resident Agency. In 1987, he transferred to the New York Field Office, where he worked on a counterintelligence squad covering Russian matters. Pitts first volunteered his services to the KGB during this assignment.

Around 1995, Rollan Dzhikiya retired from the Russian Ministry of Foreign Affairs and took a commercial job for a Moscow company in New York.

Dzhikiya had no desire to return to Russia following the demise of the USSR and wanted to cement his status in the United States. Dzhikiya knew he had something to peddle to the U.S. government to facilitate his request to stay in the country permanently and subsequently gave up the name of FBI Agent Earl Pitts.[100]

Disgruntled about his new assignment, Pitts felt unappreciated. He and his wife found a house within his salary range in Greenwood Lake, New

York, but it left him a two-hour commute from his office. Overextended in debt, he had "an overwhelming urge to lash out and strike out. I realized at that time that the way to hurt the FBI was to screw with its secrets. I wanted to get my punches in. I wanted to hurt them." How he became a traitor was more pronounced.

"It happened exceedingly early one morning. I was lying there awake, and working for the KGB suddenly changed over from being an abstract possibility to something that could really be done. It was almost like it became a given that this would happen. It became like any other operation had to be. I had to consider what the upside and the downside was....How to carry it forward became a practical problem."[101]

Pitts had then been working in FCI—foreign counterintelligence—in the FBI's New York bureau for only five months, trailing KGB agents working out of the Soviet mission at the United Nations. The Cold War was showing signs of waning, but within the bureau, hatred of the Soviets had not diminished. Russian diplomats had license plates with the code FC, which to FBI agents stood for "F—— Commies."

In 1989, Pitts was promoted to supervisory special agent and transferred to FBI Headquarters in Washington, D.C. He continued to meet with the Russians for more than two years. As part of the Bureau's arrest plan, Pitts was invited to a meeting and was greeted by two special agents, who soon confronted Pitts about his espionage. Pitts was then advised of his rights and arrested. During FBI questioning in June 1997, Pitts said that he suspected Robert Hanssen might be "trying to collect information covertly."[102]

The recounting of Pitts's questioning arose as Robert Hanssen was arrested for espionage for Russia and the Soviet Union in 2001. Pitts said he first became suspicious in the early 1990s when he learned that Hanssen had tried to gain access, without authorization, to information in the computer of another counterintelligence agent. Although Pitts was not sure that Hanssen was spying for Russia, he recounted the computer hacking to an interrogator when asked if he believed anyone else in the Bureau might be working for Moscow. The FBI let the matter pass, as they were satisfied with an initial investigation.

In January 1997, Earl Pitts pleaded guilty to espionage, and on June 23, 1997, he was sentenced to twenty-seven years in prison in Ashland, Kentucky. He was released in 2019.

JOHN WALKER JR.

In 1985, dubbed by the press as the "Year of the Spy," former U.S. Navy warrant officer John Anthony Walker Jr. was arrested for selling U.S. secrets to the Soviet Union. Walker's espionage began in 1967 when he walked into the Soviet Embassy in Washington, D.C., with material that would allow the Soviets to read encrypted naval messages.

During Walker's time as an active spy, the Soviets went as far as to give him a device that, when placed on top of a cryptographic machine, could record the rotor settings, thus allowing the Soviets to decipher all communication sent using the machines. Among the information Walker provided the Soviets was naval cryptographic technology.

Walker also recruited others to spy for the Soviet Union, including a close friend and his own family members. He even encouraged his brother and his children to join the armed services to gain access to classified material. After Walker left the Navy, his friend Jerry Whitworth continued to provide classified information from the inside regarding U.S. naval submarines. Additionally, Walker recruited his older brother Arthur and his son Michael to collect and provide him with information he could pass along to the Soviets.

Early in 1985, the FBI learned of Walker's connections to the Soviets. Using court-authorized surveillance techniques, the FBI learned Walker was planning to conduct a dead drop, a spy technique where a package of stolen secrets is hidden in a public area by the spy so that an enemy agent can pick it up at a later time, allowing people to covertly pass information between themselves without meeting face-to-face. The FBI initiated 24/7 surveillance on Walker. When he drove from Virginia to Maryland on May 19, 1985, the FBI followed him. Following the instructions his Soviet case officer had given him, he set a dead drop for the Soviets to pick up in Montgomery County, Maryland. The FBI retrieved this package and found it contained information about sensitive U.S. military technology.

John Anthony Walker was arrested at his hotel early the next morning. By early June, his three other accomplices—Jerry Whitworth, Arthur Walker and Michael Walker—were also in federal custody. John and Arthur Walker were each sentenced to life in prison. Michael Walker was sentenced to 25 years in prison and was paroled in 2000, and Jerry Whitworth was sentenced to 365 years and a fine.[103]

ROBERT HANSSEN

Robert Hanssen was born as an only child to Howard and Vivian Hanssen in the Norwood Park neighborhood of Chicago on April 18, 1944. Howard was serving as a petty officer in the Navy during the Second World War when Robert was born. Howard was a Chicago police officer, and right before Robert joined the force, Howard was a district commander in Norwood Park, which was closest to home, to be with his family.

Despite having a difficult relationship with his father, Robert Hanssen followed Howard's footsteps in the Chicago Police Department in October 1972, a few months after Howard retired from the force. During his tenure in the Chicago Police Department, Robert was assigned to the surveillance unit investigating corruption by other police officers, despite his not having ever worked as a beat cop.

Howard had always wanted his son to be a doctor. Robert obliged at least partially by enrolling in dental school at Northwestern University after attending undergraduate school at Knox College in Galesburg, Illinois. After finishing dental school, Robert decided to venture into business education and earned an MBA and CPA. He desired a position in the National Security Agency but was rejected. Soon thereafter he took a position in counter-surveillance with the Federal Bureau of Investigation.[104]

Like Father, Like Son

Surveillance ran in the family, with both Robert and his father, Howard. Howard became involved in the notorious Chicago Red Squad during the 1950s and '60s under Mayor Richard Daley, which resulted in unapproved methods to infiltrate and use illegal domestic surveillance on elements of the city that were aggressive and dangerously Communist and Socialist in nature. In the 1960s, the Peace Movement evolved into wide-ranging protests against the war in Vietnam. Chicago was especially a hotbed of activity involving mostly peaceful demonstrations but turned violent in some incidents, including the Days of Rage in 1967. As protesters turned more violent, from Students for a Democratic Society to its splinter group the Weathermen, surveillance and informants were placed within those cells and gathered intelligence that could conceivably harm not just property but people as well. The Weathermen especially were linked to violent methods, having taken credit for blowing up the Pentagon and

Capitol building in Washington, D.C., and many other targets, including a monument to police officers in recognition of their work against the Haymarket Affair rioters in 1886.

Red Squads were in full use in larger police departments in Chicago, Los Angeles and New York City. Surveillance methods against anarchist and militant labor unions in Chicago were present as early as the Haymarket Affair in 1886. In 1904, New York City undertook increased watchfulness with Italian immigrants suspected as members of gangs and the mob. Red Squads turned their full attention to suspected Communists starting in the 1930s as Stalin tightened his grip in Russia and kept full rein on organizations such as the Communist Party USA. Finally, this course of action ceased to be useful to the Bureau. Howard Hanssen was involved in a suspicious 1974 fire in the records room of the police department. The fire broke out in the area where files were housed, and the scenario itself became suspicious when only the file cabinets that housed Red Squad materials and investigations caught fire (none of the adjacent files were touched).

Robert Hanssen's Career with the FBI

FBI agent Robert Hanssen. *FBI file photo.*

As Hanssen's stint with the Chicago Police Department drew to a close in 1975, he was offered a job with counterintelligence with the FBI. He was assigned to the Midwest office of the FBI located in Gary, Indiana. Looking for a bigger assignment, Hanssen was eventually transferred to the New York City branch in 1979, where he developed the first counterintelligence database for the FBI. Just eight months after assuming his position in New York City, he delivered a package to the GRU, or military espionage wing of the Soviet Union. Having known all of the technological equipment and methods of the FBI, plus working as a CPA, Hanssen went nearly undetected until his arrest in 2001. He was arrested just two months shy of his mandatory retirement date.[105]

A damning conclusion of Robert Hanssen's activities was found in "A Review of the FBI's Performance in Deterring, Detecting, and Investigating the Espionage Activities of Robert Philip Hanssen," compiled by the Office of the Inspector General in August 2003. Hanssen's espionage spanned three separate periods: 1979–81, 1985–91 and 1999–2001. Over more than twenty years, Hanssen compromised some of this nation's most important counterintelligence and military secrets, including the identities of dozens of human sources, at least three of whom were executed. Hanssen gave the KGB thousands of pages of highly classified documents and dozens of computer disks detailing U.S. strategies in the event of nuclear war, major developments in military weapons technologies, information on active espionage cases and many other aspects of the U.S. Intelligence Community's Soviet counterintelligence program. In 1979, his wife, Bonnie, noticed him writing letters in his den. Assuming it was an affair, she confronted Robert about infidelity. Little did she expect to hear that he was actually spying. He went to confession as early as 1980 to admit to his espionage. Since clergy are by no means under duty to report confessions to the authorities, it went unknown for decades.

In the early 1980s, Hanssen served in the Budget Unit and in the Soviet Analytical Unit at FBI Headquarters in Virginia—positions that provided him with broad access to sensitive information and an opportunity to use his technical and computer skills but did not require operational work. Because the Budget Unit was responsible for preparing materials justifying the FBI's budget requests to Congress, Hanssen obtained access to sensitive information from all components of the Intelligence Division and worked closely with the NSA and the CIA to secure joint funding for certain projects. In the Soviet Analytical Unit, Hanssen gained access to the FBI's most sensitive human assets and technical operations against the Soviet Union. He also began a noticeable pattern of mishandling classified information, primarily by disclosing the existence of Soviet sources and investigations to people with no "need to know," such as FBI employees in other divisions and personnel from other agencies. While Hanssen's tours in the Budget and Soviet Analytical Units showed that he was an intelligent, analytical agent with significant computer skills, his performance also revealed that he lacked the people skills to communicate effectively and perform supervisory duties. Nonetheless, Hanssen's career at the FBI continued to advance. In the meantime, Hanssen revealed dozens of secrets during his stint spying for the Soviet Union. This included the eavesdropping tunnel the FBI had dug under the Soviet Embassy in Washington and the identities of two FBI sources within the embassy, who were also executed.[106]

In 1985, Hanssen returned to the New York office as the supervisor of a technical surveillance squad. Hanssen was a lackadaisical manager who did not interact effectively with his subordinates. Because the squad largely "ran itself," however, Hanssen's limited interpersonal skills did not become a significant issue. Similarly, Hanssen's mishandling of classified information was obvious to his subordinates but was not brought to the attention of his superiors.

1985: YEAR OF THE SPY

Hanssen paused his espionage activities before restarting in 1985, the same year multiple high-level traitors offered their services to the Soviet Union. John Walker was apprehended for sending naval information to the Soviets for nearly eighteen years. Jonathon Pollack provided information to the KGB, insisting the information would assist Israel. Perhaps the most notorious, Aldrich Ames, also offered his services as a CIA officer to the Soviets. Robert Hanssen returned to this world while others gave invaluable information that put countless agents working both for the United States and against the Cold War enemy of the Soviet Union at risk.

Hanssen pleaded guilty to fifteen counts of espionage in 2001 and was apprehended at the "Ellis" drop site—under a footbridge over Wolftrap Creek near Creek Crossing Road at Foxstone Park near Vienna, Virginia. There he clandestinely placed a package containing highly classified information for pickup by his Russian handlers.[107] He was sentenced to life in prison without any chance of parole. Robert Hanssen died in June 2023.

MOLES IN THE CIA: THE CASE OF ALDRICH AMES

Born in River Falls, Wisconsin, Aldrich "Rick" Ames moved to Northern Virginia, where he graduated from McLean High School. His father took a job with the CIA working for the Directorate of Operations (DO) in 1952. The elder Ames had one overseas tour, accompanied by his family, including Rick, in Southeast Asia from 1953 to 1955. CIA records show that Carleton Ames received a particularly negative performance appraisal from this tour and that the elder Ames had a serious alcohol dependency. Carleton Ames returned to CIA Headquarters after his overseas tour and, after a six-month probationary period, remained in the Directorate of Operations until his retirement from the CIA in 1967 at the age of sixty-two.[108]

In 1957, after his sophomore year at McLean High School, Rick Ames secured a summer job at the CIA. In the summer of 1960, he again obtained employment at the CIA, working as a laborer/ painter at a facility in Virginia. Ames remained a document analyst at the Agency within the Directorate of Operations for the next five years while attending George Washington University on both a part-time and full-time basis.

Ames was accompanied by his first wife, Nancy Segebarth, who was also an employee of the Agency, to Turkey, where he worked as an operations officer. Nancy was required to resign from the Agency but continued to perform part-time administrative work in her husband's office.

Aldrich Ames in a high school photo. *McLean High School 1958 Yearbook.*

During his first year in Ankara, Ames was rated as a "strong" performer and promoted in 1970. By the end of the third year, Ames's superiors considered him unsuited for field work and expressed the view that perhaps he should spend the remainder of his career at CIA Headquarters in Langley, a devastating assessment for an operations officer.

Beginning in 1972, he was assigned to Soviet- and Iron Curtain–related cases with the CIA and learned the Russian language. Ames was assigned to New York City from 1976 until 1981, where he managed two important Soviet assets for the CIA. Ames's inattention to detail led to two significant security violations during this period. In an incident that occurred in 1976 when Ames was on his way to meet a Soviet asset, he left his briefcase on a subway train. The briefcase contained classified operational materials that could have compromised the Soviet asset concerned. Within hours, the FBI had retrieved the briefcase from the Polish émigré who found it, but it was unclear to what extent the information may have been compromised. In October 1980, Ames was cited for leaving top secret communications equipment unsecured in his office. But this also did not result in an official reprimand.

In 1982, he met his future wife, Rosario, at the Colombian Embassy in Mexico City. Ames's relationship with Rosario grew increasingly serious until he eventually proposed marriage to her. They married in 1984. Despite Agency regulations, Ames did not report his romance with a foreign national to his superiors. Some of Ames's colleagues were aware of the relationship, but this did not prompt him to file the necessary report.

When Ames returned to headquarters in September 1983, he was made counterintelligence branch chief for Soviet operations, responsible for analyzing selected CIA operations involving Soviet "assets." In this counterintelligence function, Ames was in a position to gain access to all CIA operations involving Soviet intelligence officers worldwide. His assignment also gave him access to all CIA plans and operations targeted against the KGB and GRU intelligence services.

In 1985, Rick Ames recruited himself. He sold a Soviet Embassy official the names of two KGB officers secretly working for the FBI in Washington. His asking price for the information was $50,000. The next month, he volunteered the names of every Soviet intelligence official and military officer he knew was working for the United States, along with whatever else he knew about CIA operations against Moscow. In September of that year, shortly after he and Rosario married, he received a wedding present from the KGB in the amount of $2 million. He claims he was shocked, and the money was far more than any other American spy is known to have received from the Soviet Union.[109]

The CIA had known since early 1986 that there was a traitor within. Employees filed complaints with their superiors that Ames was living beyond the means of any Central Intelligence Agency employee and that his wife was not as wealthy as he claimed. In 1986 and 1991, he was forced to take a polygraph lie-detector test. He feared he would not pass it. His KGB handlers told him to just remain calm while taking the test. Ames passed the test both times with no problem.

In response to suspicions of Ames, the CIA transferred him to Rome in 1986, where he stayed until 1988, working for the CIA's Soviet Counterintelligence Division. Yet he continued selling secrets to the KGB. Although Ames's job was allegedly to recruit Soviet agents into the CIA, he failed to successfully recruit a single Soviet agent. His work, however, provided him with the names of Soviet informants, and it was this information he sold to the KGB. By 1989, after his return to the United States, he had made enough money to pay cash for a $540,000 home in Arlington, Virginia.

Both the CIA and FBI were slowly learning that Soviet officials who had been recruited by them were being arrested and executed. These officials had provided critical intelligence information about the Soviet Union, which was used by U.S. policymakers in determining policy against the Soviet Union and other countries during the Cold War.[110]

Following analytical reviews and receipt of information about Ames's unexplained wealth, the FBI opened an investigation in May 1993. FBI special agents and investigative specialists conducted intensive physical and electronic surveillance of Ames during a ten-month investigation. Searches of Ames's residence revealed documents and other information linking Ames to the Russian foreign intelligence service. On October 13, 1993, investigative specialists observed a chalk mark Ames made on a mailbox confirming to the Russians his intention to meet them in Bogotá, Colombia. This mailbox is on display at the International Spy Museum in Washington, D.C.

On November 1, special agents observed him and, separately, his Russian handler in Bogotá. When Ames planned foreign travel, including a trip to Moscow, as part of his official duties, a plan to arrest him was approved.[111]

He was convicted and sentenced to life in prison in a medium-security Federal Correctional Institution (FCI) in Terre Haute, Indiana.

10

GENERAL GEORGE C. MARSHALL
AND THE MARSHALL PLAN

George C. Marshall was born in Uniontown, Pennsylvania. His family had strong roots in Virginia, where Marshall returned to attend the Virginia Military Institute. Following his graduation in 1901, he received his commission as second lieutenant in the U.S. Army. Marshall enjoyed an extremely successful military career, serving in both world wars and rising to the rank of five-star general in 1944.

During the Second World War, Marshall distinguished himself as Army Chief of Staff, a position to which he was appointed by President Franklin D. Roosevelt. As chief of staff, Marshall earned a formidable reputation as an administrator and successfully transformed a small peacetime army into a strong wartime force while also coordinating Allied operations.

After his resignation speech at the Pentagon in November 1945, George and his wife, Katherine, headed to Leesburg to Dodona Manor. Several hours later, the White House called George Marshall with immediate urgency. President Truman said to him, "Without any preparation, I told him: General, I want you to go to China for me. Marshall said only 'Yes, Mr. President,' and hung up abruptly." Marshall was designated special ambassadorial envoy to China and left immediately, with his wife, Katherine, at a standstill after just unpacking belongings, believing they were to leave his professional duties behind. Instead, Marshall was to intercede in a much concerning civil war between Mao Tse Tung's Communists and the Nationalist KMT government of Chiang Kai-shek. Marshall had been thrust into the situation due to the sudden departure of the ambassador to

Above: George C. Marshall with General John Pershing. *Library of Congress.*

Right: George C. Marshall. *U.S. Army photo.*

China, Patrick J. Hurley, with the latter warning of Chinese Communist sympathizers in the White House.[112]

Marshall, it would appear, had appeased the Communists and undermined the Nationalists during his visit. Detractors insisted Marshall had contributed to losing China. He was also said to have returned Zhou Enlai's diary to him without inspecting its contents and passing along to American intelligence, which later revealed sensitive information as to the Chinese Communist Party (CCP) troop strength and intelligence contacts within the KMT. Mao and the CCP had never intended to honor any ceasefire agreement that would give up leverage, nor any military integration with the KMT Nationalist Army for a unified China. In deference to Vladimir Lenin's assessment of treaties with the Soviet Union, a Communist's view of agreements on paper was as good as ignored when the ink dried. By the time Marshall returned to the United States, the situation in Manchuria had deteriorated. After the Soviets withdrew, the CCP moved in, and street fighting ensued. Eventually, Marshall convinced Kai-shek to agree to a ceasefire in Manchuria. Years later, Marshall would admit that the agreement was a mistake and had been the last chance to defeat the CCP army for good.[113]

Marshall, upon leaving China, was nominated to become secretary of state. This was immediately after his deduction that it was a lost cause trying to negotiate a coalition government between the Communists and KMT. Despite this criticism, Marshall was unanimously approved by the newly elected Republican Senate. There was concern that a military officer was taking on a civilian position. At the time, the secretary of state was next in line to assume the presidency after the vice president. FDR's passing in 1945 was fresh in the minds of policymakers, and the law was changed to make the speaker of the House the next in line in 1947.

China officially fell to the Communists in 1948. The Nationalists fled to Formosa (now Taiwan), and as of this writing, it continues to be a policy of China to recognize Taiwan as part of "One China." Along with the Soviet Union's detonation of an atomic bomb in 1949, the Truman administration was rightly under criticism for not doing enough to combat the march of Communism in Asia. With Stalin's Soviet troops remaining in Eastern and Central Europe, along with strong Communist groups arising in France, Greece and Italy, among others, there was indignation that not enough was being done to contain the spread of this insidious political ideology.

In all fairness, Marshall did not have much in terms of leverage, especially after military intervention was taken off the table immediately by Truman. His biggest blunder was taking the Communists' words at face value, which was known while dealing with Mao's backers in the Soviet Union. This lesson would change his tactics, however, after taking over as head of the State Department. His first hire for the policy planning division was George Kennan, America's foremost Soviet expert since the USSR's founding in the 1920s. More recently, Kennan had been named ambassador to the Soviet Union before being expelled by Stalin. Kennan had noticeably criticized the Soviet Union's return to a closed society, a departure from its Allied involvement during the war.

In 1946, Kennan, as deputy chief of mission at the United States Embassy in Moscow, issued a cable to Washington, D.C. The cable outlined and highlighted the Soviet outlook in the postwar period and how to combat Soviet Communist advance. This Long Telegram would become the United States' basic foreign policy against the Soviet Union and the world for nearly sixty years. The Long Telegram was summarized and published in *Foreign Affairs* in July 1947 as "The Sources of Soviet Conduct." Kennan's article, signed as "X" for anonymity, outlined and formulated the Containment Policy. Containment would come to be defined as taking on the Soviet Union and Communist expansion through less direct methods other than warfare between the two superpowers. However, containment would also lead to accepting the existing fate of millions of citizens inside countries behind the Iron Curtain in Europe. In order to solve that problem, Kennan and others devised Operation Rollback.

Kennan surmised that as the Containment Policy was being formulated, something needed to be done quickly in order to help Europe's reconstruction efforts and deny Communist gains in those countries. Based on Kennan's advice, Harry Truman and Secretary of State George Marshall devised a plan designed to give aid to and rebuild Europe and other devastated nations. It was a plan and economic offering keen to keep the Communists from gaining power in Europe as well. Communist parties were strongly active in Italy, Greece, France and other nations of Europe. The Economic Cooperation Plan (otherwise known as the Marshall Plan) passed the U.S. Congress in April 1948.[114]

In order to disburse and accept foreign aid to rebuild their economies and infrastructure, countries had to join the recently created Organization for European Economic Co-operation (OEEC) in 1948. The Soviet Union and its satellite countries were also offered aid but refused. Czechoslovakia, Poland and Hungary showed interest in the plan, but the Soviet Union brought pressure on them not to participate and countered with its own economic program for Eastern Europe.

One secretive provision of the Marshall Plan was that 5 percent of these funds would be withheld and used by the Central Intelligence Agency to fund Operation Rollback efforts. Funds would be paid in local currencies for unspecified purposes (such as embassy upkeep). Money flowed to rollback efforts. Funds to support guerrilla and popular revolt uprising then would be utilized in the Baltic Republics, Poland, Albania and other Iron Curtain countries to destabilize and weaken Soviet occupation and Soviet puppet governments. Operation Rollback was to recruit refugees from war-torn Europe for training otherwise tough fighters to create those popular uprisings and roll back the Soviet advances of the Second World War. Four aims of the program were psychological warfare; political warfare, such as underground resistance support and encouraging defection; economic warfare to include market manipulation, black market and counterfeiting; and finally direct action, implemented through guerrilla sabotage demolition (see chapter 7 for more information).

Meanwhile, the Truman Doctrine in 1947 laid down the response of America during the early years of the Cold War. With Great Britain financially unable to prop up its concerns in the Middle East and Mediterranean, the British approached the United States to assist in both Greek infighting with Communists and Turkey in the Dardanelle Straits.[115] The Truman Doctrine was bold in that it sent a message to those in danger of Communist expansion anywhere around the globe.

President Truman outlined the immediate threat that Communist partisans undertook in Greece and neighboring countries:

The very existence of the Greek state is today threatened by the terrorist activities of several thousand armed men, led by Communists, who defy the government's authority at a number of points, particularly along the northern boundaries. A Commission appointed by the United Nations Security Council is at present investigating disturbed conditions in northern Greece and alleged border violations along the frontier between Greece on the one hand and Albania, Bulgaria, and Yugoslavia on the other.

Meanwhile, the Greek Government is unable to cope with the situation. The Greek army is small and poorly equipped. It needs supplies and equipment if it is to restore the authority of the government throughout Greek territory. Greece must have assistance if it is to become a self-supporting and self-respecting democracy.

The United States must supply that assistance. We have already extended to Greece certain types of relief and economic aid but these are inadequate.

Truman went on to include the situation in Turkey:

Greece's neighbor, Turkey, also deserves our attention.

The future of Turkey as an independent and economically sound state is clearly no less important to the freedom-loving peoples of the world than the future of Greece. The circumstances in which Turkey finds itself today are considerably different from those of Greece. Turkey has been spared the disasters that have beset Greece. And during the war, the United States and Great Britain furnished Turkey with material aid.

The peoples of a number of countries of the world have recently had totalitarian regimes forced upon them against their will. The Government of the United States has made frequent protests against coercion and intimidation, in violation of the Yalta agreement, in Poland, Rumania, and Bulgaria. I must also state that in a number of other countries there have been similar developments.

At the present moment in world history nearly every nation must choose between alternative ways of life. The choice is too often not a free one.

One way of life is based upon the will of the majority, and is distinguished by free institutions, representative government, free elections, guarantees of individual liberty, freedom of speech and religion, and freedom from political oppression.

The second way of life is based upon the will of a minority forcibly imposed upon the majority. It relies upon terror and oppression, a controlled press and radio, fixed elections, and the suppression of personal freedoms.

I believe that it must be the policy of the United States to support free peoples who are resisting attempted subjugation by armed minorities or by outside pressures.

A $400 million aid package was approved for assistance in those countries. After a conference in Moscow with the Allied powers discussing items ranging from elections to German reparations, it became clear the Soviets did not want any resurgence of Germany or other Western European economies for two reasons. First, it would weaken those countries and make them more susceptible to Soviet influence and dominance. Second, it would satiate the appetite for the Soviets to see that their neighbors, especially Germany, would not be strong enough to attack Russia, as it had twice in the twentieth century up to that point. Marshall then sensed another line of assistance needed to be considered to assist Europe's recovery. It would soon become known as the Marshall Plan, as Truman's name was anathema to the new Republican Congress.

While the Marshall Plan was extended to any European country in need, it became clear that Stalin and the Soviet Union did not want their satellite states to be involved whatsoever. Stalin viewed the plan as dividing Europe and isolating the Soviet Union. Likewise, Stalin insisted that the Eastern European countries under Soviet occupation not attend the Paris convention and made it clear he was in favor of dividing Europe. The battle lines of the Cold War had thus been drawn—those receiving aid and those refusing it.

Accepting the premise of the Marshall Plan also hastened the cooperation and consolidation of Western powers in Germany. Heretofore there were American, British and French zones occupying that country. To promote trade and strengthen the economy, the zones were then consolidated. The European Cooperation Act of 1948, as the Marshall Plan bill was titled, continued in earnest until 1951, as the funds were terminated in light of the Korean War. Military spending and defense of Europe took higher priority as well. At the same time the price tag of the Marshall Plan was being debated, the idea of NATO was started as a joint venture with Britain and other Western European countries.

DODONA MANOR, LEESBURG, VIRGINIA

George C. Marshall's Dodona Manor is situated on 3.8 acres of gardens on the eastern end of Leesburg's Old and Historic District. The site is designated a National Historic Landmark as the residence of General

Dodona Manor, weekend retreat of George C. Marshall and his wife, Leesburg, Virginia. *Library of Congress.*

George C. Marshall from 1941 to 1959. General Marshall was described as the "greatest American of the twentieth century" by both Franklin Roosevelt and Winston Churchill. More than 90 percent of the items in the house belonged to the Marshalls when they lived here in the 1950s.[116]

Marshall resigned as secretary of state in 1949 and became president of the American Red Cross. However, he returned to the Truman Cabinet as secretary of defense in 1950 and served briefly in that capacity until 1951. Marshall died in 1959 after receiving the Nobel Peace Prize in 1953 for his work to restore Europe's economy in the post–World War II period.

11

FRANCIS GARY POWERS AND THE U-2 INCIDENT

Francis Gary Powers was born to Oliver and Ida Powers on August 17, 1929, in Burdine, Kentucky, and raised in Pound, Virginia.[117] He grew up during the Great Depression and graduated in 1946 from Grundy High School in Virginia. Four years later, in 1950, he graduated from Milligan College in Tennessee and enlisted in the U.S. Air Force as an aviation cadet. Powers maintained the Virginia domicile from 1929 to 1963, when he relocated to California to work as a test pilot for Lockheed Aircraft Corporation.

MILITARY SERVICE AND CAREER OVERVIEW

Francis Gary Powers received his wings and commission in December 1952 and flew F-84s until he was recruited in May 1956 to become a U-2 pilot for the CIA on a joint U.S. Air Force program. He began high-altitude surveillance and overflights of the USSR in 1956, which provided vital intelligence photographs of Russian military activity to the Eisenhower administration. On May 1, 1960, Powers was shot down over Sverdlovsk, USSR, by a newly developed SA-2 missile. Powers was captured, sentenced and held prisoner until his exchange on February 10, 1962, for Russian KGB spy Colonel Rudolf Abel. The incident was depicted in Steven Spielberg's Cold War thriller *Bridge of Spies*.

Following his return to the United States in February 1962, Powers was extensively debriefed by the U.S. government, awarded the CIA's Intelligence Star for Valor and shown "to be a fine young man performing well under dangerous circumstances" by the Senate Select Committee assembled to investigate the U-2 Incident. Within months of his return home, his marriage fell apart; he and his first wife divorced, and in October 1963, he married Claudia "Sue" Edwards.

Powers flew for Lockheed as a U-2 test pilot from late 1963 until early 1970. He played a vital role as a Lockheed test pilot to ensure that U-2 planes were ready for deployment for operational missions around the world. In 1970, he published

Francis Gary Powers's official Air Force photo. *Courtesy of www. GaryPowers.com.*

his book, *Operation Overflight*, which detailed his account of the U-2 Incident. From 1972 to 1977, he flew for radio stations KGIL and K-NBC News Channel 4 in Los Angeles, doing on-air weather, news and traffic reports. He was killed in a helicopter crash on August 1, 1977, in Encino, California, while news reporting for K-NBC News Channel 4. Powers is the father of Dee Powers and Francis Gary Powers Jr. He is buried at Arlington National Cemetery in Virginia.

Although Captain Powers was initially criticized (some believed that he should have killed himself rather than be captured), a 1998 joint CIA and Air Force declassification conference held at Fort McNair in Washington, D.C., showed that Powers followed orders by maintaining a cooperative attitude, gave out no secret information and refused to denounce the United States of America. On May 1, 2000, as a result of the 1998 declassification conference showing military service at the time of the U-2 Incident, Powers was posthumously awarded the National Defense Service Medal, the Prisoner of War Medal, the Distinguished Flying Cross and the CIA's Director's Medal for "Extreme Fidelity and Courage" in the line of duty. On June 15, 2012, the U.S. Air Force awarded Powers the Silver Star for valor in the line of duty while he was incarcerated in the Soviet Union.

Powers was included in the *Virginians on Time Magazine* display at the Virginia Historical Society, and in 2010, a Francis Gary Powers U-2

Right: Francis Gary Powers poses with an F-84 Thunderjet. *Courtesy of www. GaryPowers.com.*

Below: U-2 squadron. Francis Gary Powers is top left. *Courtesy of www. GaryPowers.com.*

Francis Gary Powers seated inside an F-84. *Courtesy of www.GaryPowers.com.*

Incident exhibit was displayed there. In July 2007, the Commonwealth of Virginia erected a historic marker in Pound, Virginia, in recognition of Francis Gary Powers's service to the United States during the Cold War, and in March 2016, the Wise County Lonesome Pine Airport's terminal was renamed in his honor.

VIRGINIA HISTORICAL MARKER VERBIAGE

Dedicated July 2007 in Pound, Virginia:

U-2 Pilot Francis Gary Powers (1929–1977), raised in Pound, Virginia, upon graduating from Grundy High School attended Milligan College. In 1956, after six years in the USAF the CIA recruited Powers to fly espionage missions over the Soviet Union. On May 1, 1960 the Soviets shot down his U-2 spy plane. Eventually captured,

Powers stated his compass had malfunctioned on a weather flight. Finding film intact in the wreckage, he was sentenced to ten years for espionage. Powers was exchanged on February 10, 1962 for a Soviet spy. Powers, who later flew for Los Angeles radio and TV stations reporting on weather and traffic, died August 1, 1977 in a helicopter crash. Posthumously decorated by the CIA and USAF he is buried in Arlington National Cemetery.

SETTING THE RECORD STRAIGHT

On May 1, 2015, the fifty-fifth anniversary of the U-2 Incident, Francis Gary Powers Jr. spoke about his father's legacy and growing up as the son of the famed U-2 pilot:

Fifty-five years after my father was shot down over the former Soviet Union, I still find it interesting that people who know very little about my father, the U-2 Incident, his actions or inactions, are usually the first to post comments to newsgroups, blogs and or write editorials or articles that continue to circulate misinformation, disrespect my father and contradict the truth of what has been determined over the past fifty-five years through declassified documents, CIA/USAF history conferences, and official US/ USSR military reports.

As a result of my father being unable to stand up for himself while imprisoned in the former Soviet Union (and after his death), there were many editorials written in newspapers and reported in the media about my father's actions...how he supposedly had a flame out, defected, landed the plane intact, and or spilled his guts and told the KGB everything he knew.

For the record, on May 1, 1960, Powers was shot down at his assigned altitude of 70,500 feet over Sverdlovsk, USSR, by a newly developed Soviet SA-2 missile. There was no sabotage, no flame out and no conspiracy to ruin the May 16 Paris Summit Conference. After bailing out of the aircraft at thirty thousand feet, his parachute opened at fifteen thousand feet, and Powers parachuted down to the ground, where he was caught and turned over to the KGB. After being captured, Powers was interrogated for three months in the KGB Lubyanka Prison, tried August 17 at the Hall of Columns and sentenced August 19 to ten years in Soviet prison.

Better relations through trade. Exchange of Francis Gary Powers and Colonel Rudolf Abel in 1962. *Library of Congress.*

He was held prisoner for a total of twenty-one months until his exchange at the Glienicke Bridge on February 10, 1962, for Russian spy Colonel Rudolf Abel, who was caught in the late 1950s in New York City. Although Captain Powers has been criticized at times for "living through" the ordeal by some in the American government, the media and veteran groups, 1998 declassified documents show that he was not under orders to commit suicide if captured, gave out no secret information to the enemy and refused to denounce the United States of America at his show trial. As a result, Soviet intelligence gained no vital information from him during his twenty-one months of captivity.

Powers is buried at Arlington National Cemetery in Virginia.

Here follows the list of awards and decorations received by Francis Gary Powers as a result of his U.S. Air Force and CIA aviation career.

CIA Intelligence Star for Valor (April 20, 1965)
CIA Director's Award for Extreme Fidelity and Courage (May 1, 2000)

USAF Distinguished Flying Cross (May 1, 2000)
Prisoner of War Medal (May 1, 2000)
National Defense Service Medal (May 1, 2000)
USAF Silver Star (June 15, 2012)

"Citation to Accompany Award of the Distinguished Flying Cross to Francis Gary Powers"

This document states:

> *Captain Francis G. Powers distinguished himself by extraordinary achievement while participating in aerial flight as a U-2 pilot assigned to Turkey on 1 May 1960. Flying under extremely hazardous conditions, Captain Powers was able to penetrate denied territory providing support to the joint United States Air Force-Agency U-2 Program. The professional competence, aerial skill, and devotion to duty displayed by Captain Powers reflect great credit upon himself and the United States Air Force.*

"Citation to Accompany Award of the Silver Star to Francis Gary Powers"

This document states:

> *The President of the United States of America, authorized by Act of Congress July 9, 1918 (amended by an act of July 25, 1963), takes pride in presenting the Silver Star (Posthumously) to Captain Francis Gary Powers, United States Air Force, for gallantry in connection with military operations against an armed enemy of the United States from 1 May 1960 to 10 February 1962. During this period, while assigned to the Joint United States Air Force, Central Intelligence Agency, U-2 Reconnaissance Squadron, Detachment 10-10, Captain Powers was held captive in solitary confinement in the infamous Lubyanka Prison, Moscow, in the former Union of Soviet Socialist Republics, after his U-2 aircraft had been shot down by a Soviet surface to air missile over enemy territory. For almost 107 days, Captain Powers was interrogated, harassed, and endured unmentionable hardships on a continuous basis by numerous top Soviet Secret Police interrogating teams. Although greatly weakened*

physically by the lack of food, denial of sleep and the mental rigors of constant interrogation, Captain Powers steadfastly refused all attempts to give sensitive defense information or be exploited for propaganda purposes, resisting all Soviet efforts through cajolery, trickery, and threats of death to obtain the confessions they sought as part of the pretrial investigation. Captain Powers was subjected to an international trial and was sentenced to an additional 542 days of captivity in Vladimir Prison before finally being released to United States control. As a result of his indomitable spirit, exceptional loyalty, and continuous heroic actions, Russian intelligence gained no vital information from him. For his sustained courage in an exceptionally hostile environment, Captain Powers was publicly recognized by the Director of the Central Intelligence Agency and the Senate Armed Services Committee. By his gallantry and devotion to duty in the dedication of his service to his country, Captain Powers has reflected great credit upon himself and the United States Air Force.[118]

The Cold War lasted for another thirty-one years after my father was shot down over the Soviet Union. The U-2 Incident forced the U.S. government to admit publicly that there was a worldwide intelligence network operated by the Central Intelligence Agency that was able to penetrate the Soviet Union. This effort, in the words of President Eisenhower, was "a vital but distasteful necessity in order to avert another Pearl Harbor."

Although my father's flight—the twenty-fourth over the Soviet Union—was the last to overfly that country, U-2s continued to fly reconnaissance missions over Cuba, the Middle East, China, Southeast Asia and parts of Africa, Kosovo and other countries as needed to protect the United States. More U-2s were shot down by SA-2 missiles, the same weapon that downed my father's aircraft on May Day 1960. Still, the U-2 flew on, with the CIA operating the aircraft until 1974, when the surviving agency U-2s were transferred to the Air Force. Sensors were upgraded, and new variants of the U-2 were produced—larger, with more powerful engines and carrying more advanced sensors. A tactical reconnaissance or TR-1 variant was developed for the direct support of a future war in Europe; however, that aircraft was merged into the strategic U-2 series. In fact, the National Aeronautics and Space administration had taken over several U-2s for scientific research. These were followed by the ER-2 variant, produced specifically for NASA operations.

At the beginning of the twenty-first century, there were U-2s making periphery flights and overflights of several crisis areas. The U-2 outlasted its planned successor, the SR-71 Blackbird, a Mach 3 aircraft that could fly higher than the U-2 and carried a sensor operator in addition to the pilot. But the SR-71 proved too expensive to operate, and the last aircraft was retired in 1990.

Not only did the U-2 outlast its planned successor, but it has continued to fly in an era of reconnaissance satellites and unmanned aircraft (UAV) as well. Indeed, there are plans for advanced unmanned aerial vehicles to eventually replace the U-2, but nothing will compare with a piloted aircraft.

The U-2 of my father's era was a highly secret aircraft, rarely photographed and never spoken of by officials. Today the details of the U-2 are widely known, with only information on some of its reconnaissance equipment and mission specifications being closely held by the government.

After his return to the United States, my father worked briefly at CIA headquarters in Langley, Virginia, near Washington, D.C., training agents on what to do if captured and how to conduct themselves during an interrogation session. One day, as my father walked around a corner, he bumped into an attractive woman—and spilt her cup of coffee over her dress. He offered to buy Sue Downey another cup and took up a conversation in which he told her that his car was going into the shop and asked if she happened to travel by Glebe Road to work. She answered

Francis Gary Powers's Senate hearing. *Library of Congress.*

in the affirmative and offered to give him a lift. In repayment, he asked her out to lunch. Lunch turned into dinner. Dinner turned into romance. They started dating while Dad and his first wife, Barbara, were separated. Dad's first marriage had been rocky from the start; the U-2 Incident, his imprisonment and the press coverage did not help the situation and soon led to their divorce in August 1963.

Dad was tired of the desk job at the CIA. Upon his return home, Kelly Johnson, designer of the U-2, had said any time Dad needed a job he had one with Lockheed. In 1963, he took Kelly up on the offer. After he was requalified in the U-2 and passed the physical and psychological exams, Dad moved to California to work for Johnson at the Lockheed Skunk Works.

Sue Downey and he had a long-distance relationship for several months. Dad asked her out to Los Angeles for a visit, and instead of a diamond ring she got two—one for each of the two years that they had known each other. He proposed within a few weeks.

In 1969, Powers started working on his autobiography, *Operation Overflight*. Shortly before it was published in early 1970, Kelly Johnson called him into his office at Burbank and informed him that there was no more work for him at Lockheed. Dad's termination from Lockheed happened the same month that the CIA was vetting his final draft of *Operation Overflight*. It seems that the Agency was willing to pay Dad's salary as long as he kept quiet, but because of the publication of *Operation Overflight*, some feathers were ruffled at Langley and my father was let go from Lockheed.

In 1972, after two years of promoting the book and appearing on the lecture and talk show circuit, my father got a job again as a pilot flying for KGIL Radio Station reporting on weather, news and traffic above Los Angeles. In 1976, he became a helicopter traffic pilot-reporter for KNBC News Channel 4. On August 1, 1977, he died in a helicopter crash while reporting on traffic over Los Angeles. My father died doing what he loved to do—flying. It was tragic for my family, but, as my mother often said, it was better than if he had died in an automobile accident on the freeway or by a slip in the tub.

I remember attending my father's funeral—at the time, I was twelve years old. The events between August 1977 and the day that I started junior high are a little blurred. Everything was in a whirlwind. I arrived home from summer school at 1:15 p.m. on August 1 after being dropped off by a friend's dad. No sooner had I set foot inside our home than Mom dragged me out again to grab a quick meal at a local restaurant and pick up a few things from the grocery store.

Francis Gary Powers with his family.
Courtesy of www.GaryPowers.com.

The car radio was broken, and Mom and I did not have an opportunity to listen to the breaking news that my father and cameraman George Spears were killed in a helicopter crash. When we arrived home, we were greeted by two close family friends, Mrs. Neff and Mrs. Marlow. Mrs. Neff was the wife of Arthur Neff, whose father was a well-known architect credited with designing the Mary Pickford Estate. Mrs. Marlow was the wife of Jess Marlow, who was the anchorman for KNBC, where my father worked.

As we pulled into the driveway, I pointed to Mrs. Neff coming out of our home and asked my mother how she had got inside. Mom answered, "She probably came in from the back waiting for us to get home." As we entered our home, Mrs. Neff said, "Sue, you had better sit down." In reply, Mom asked her to help with the groceries and they would talk in a minute. Again, Mrs. Neff said, "Sue, you had better sit down."

All of a sudden, my mom got this look on her face as if she had seen a ghost. She dropped a bag of groceries. In the background, I heard Mrs. Marlow say, "They have just arrived; I will call you back." She had been on the telephone in the study.

As the groceries dropped, I heard my mother say, "Oh my God, it's Frank. If he is alive, take me to him; if he is dead let me know." All Mrs. Neff and Mrs. Marlow could do was shake their heads and shrug their shoulders because they did not know yet or were not telling.

I found myself in my room staring out the window thinking that Dad had been in an accident and broken an arm or leg. Mrs. Neff came in and talked with me a bit, nothing that I remember other than being asked if there was a friend I would like to visit. My automatic response was Chris Conrad, a lifelong friend and son of Robert Conrad of "Wild Wild West" and "Baa Baa Black Sheep" fame. Chris and I had grown up together since the second grade, when we had met in class.

After getting Chris on the phone, Mrs. Neff drove me over to their home in Encino, California. About the time that we got there, Mrs. Conrad arrived home and asked Mrs. Neff why we were there. Mrs. Neff explained that there had been an accident. They talked alone for a while in whispers as Chris and I poked each other and then Mrs. Conrad came over and gave me a huge, gigantic bear hug. My eyes started to water, and I wiped away the tears that were forming, not realizing why I was crying and trying not to cry in front of one of my friends.

Within a half hour after Mrs. Neff had left, the phone rang at the Conrads' home. Mrs. Conrad answered, and I heard her say, "Yes, I know. Gary is here now." With that, she asked me to come to the phone because "Duke," as Bob Conrad was known, wanted to speak with me.

Mr. Conrad gave me a pep talk and told me how much my dad meant to a lot of people and some other remarks that were meant to comfort and console me. I remember him saying that my father was a great man, a true American hero, and that I should be proud to carry his name.

I think I spent the night at the Conrads' house. When I returned home, there was a large number of people there, including another good friend of my dad, Gregg Anderson, who was coordinating the activities between phone calls, burial plans, airline reservations, hotel bookings and the press. For the next several hours, different people arrived and departed the house. My sister also arrived home. She had been stationed in the Reserves at Norton Air Force Base in San Bernardino, California, for the past three years.

More family and friends arrived over the next few days. A memorial service was held, and I heard that Barbara, my dad's first wife, attended, although I do not remember her. I overheard the adults talking, saying that she had called the KNBC newsroom announcing that Mrs. Francis Gary Powers had arrived and asked that a limousine be sent to pick her up at the airport. The person who happened to answer the phone knew my mom and dad and explained that it would not be possible for a limo to be sent and that Mrs. Francis Gary Powers lived in the San Fernando Valley.

I remember riding to the memorial service with my mom, sister and two aunts and gazing out of the window as we pulled up to the church, which was overflowing with people. The limo doors opened, and I was greeted by numerous other friends and their parents. I also saw a group of news reporters with cameras and a microphone extended toward us. My mother whispered to me as we entered the church, "Don't say a word."

Family friend and KNBC news anchorman Jess Marlow gave the eulogy. I heard a lot of sobbing. It seemed to be over as quickly as it had begun, and we exited the side door only to be met by an onslaught of news reporters with their cameras and microphones. I remember wanting to jump out and step on a microphone that was being held inches from me. But my mother once again told me not to say a word and do not do anything as we walked directly toward the waiting limo. The sea of reporters parted as the limo doors were opened and we returned to our house.

The wake lasted into the early hours of the morning. I remember being downstairs in the TV room and peeking around the corner as people were watching the evening news. I saw Jess Marlow give an overview of the service and remember that he started to cry when he said that Frank would be missed by all at KNBC.

My father had told Gregg Anderson that if he were to die not to let my mother try to bury him at Arlington National Cemetery. He felt that there were too many people in the CIA and government who would not allow him to be buried there. Every time Gregg asked my mom where Frank was to be buried, she would say Arlington. Once when Gregg asked if there was an alternative, she said, "No"—only Arlington.

Gregg called CIA headquarters in Langley, Virginia. He told me later that it was the oddest experience that he ever had. Every time he called, the line would pick up, but no one would say anything until Gregg spoke first. Once Gregg had said that it was Gregg Anderson calling on behalf of the Francis Gary Powers family, the person on the other end would reply and the conversation would start.

General Leo P. Gerry, who had been the Air Force project officer for the U-2, was at the wake, and he pulled me aside and said that my father had been issued the Distinguished Flying Cross and that he would make certain that it got to us. But it was not until 1986 that we received it at an informal ceremony at a U-2 reunion in Las Vegas.

Our local congressman, Robert Dornan, assisted in getting President Carter to authorize my dad's internment in Arlington. But it was President Carter who authorized the paperwork.

We arrived at the Los Angeles International (LAX) Airport and were waiting in one of the lounges. My mother excused herself and said that she was going to check on Dad. I said I wanted to go with her, but she refused. Only several years later did I learn that she had gone down and looked inside the coffin before it was loaded onto the plane. On the flight to Dulles Airport in Virginia, we flew for the first time in first class.

Subsequently, while in the waiting room of Arlington National Cemetery prior to the burial, my mom told me that my father was being buried in a section of Arlington that was off the beaten path. It was a spot on top of a hill that the tour buses did not go by. She said it was the section of Arlington where several CIA heroes were buried. At the funeral, a man walked up to me and put a coin in my hand. He said that "Zugard" wanted me to have this. Zugard had been my dad's cellmate in prison in the Soviet Union. As I turned around to show my mom, I said, "Look what this man gave me." She asked, "What man?" When I turned around to point him out, he had disappeared into the crowd.

On the flight back to California, as I was looking out the window at a clear blue sky, there was one dark cloud in the distance. As we flew by, the dark cloud took on the shape of a silent U-2 floating in the sky. Several minutes passed, and I asked my mom if she had seen what I had seen. She shook her head yes and fought to hold back tears. I said, "Mom, don't cry. It's Dad's way of letting us know it will be alright."

Hours became days, and days became weeks, and slowly I started to recover from my heartache. My summer school history teacher, Mrs. Orr, told my mom that the spark had left my eye after the death of my father. High school was difficult for me. I attended a private high school, and many of the students, including fellow classmates, were from wealthy families. It was common to see BMWs, Mercedes and other expensive cars in the student lot. There seemed to be a lot of cliques into which I did not fit. I was neither a brain nor a jock.

Throughout high school, I was introverted. Some of my classmates or peers would come up to me and ask me about my dad, and sometimes they would tell me what they had heard from their parents about my father. This was strange, because they would know something about my family and me, but I did not know anything about them or their family. As a result, I learned to introduce myself as "Gary" so that I would not be asked, "Gary Powers, is that any relation to...?" I learned at an early age to distinguish between people who liked me for me and people who liked me because of who my father was.

I got through high school and enrolled at the local California State University, Northridge. I had wanted to attend an out-of-state school, but my mother had convinced me to enroll at CSUN to see how I liked college. After a year or so, she said, I could transfer to another school. In hindsight, one of the concerns my mother faced was how to pay for my college education. When Dad died, all income halted except for Social Security survivor's benefits. Mom never returned to work. She was able to make ends meet by investing Dad's insurance money and the savings they had accumulated.

I also received Social Security survivor benefits, which my mom used to pay for the private high school education. However, when it came time to pay for college, it turned out that President Reagan had cut back on certain programs, one of which stopped the continuation of certain Social Security benefits. As a result, my mom paid for my classes and books, and I worked part time to earn spending money.

In August 1983, between high school and college, I received a rush flyer and a schedule of events from the Sigma Alpha Epsilon Fraternity at CSUN— Cal Nu as it was known. Not knowing much about fraternities at the time, I was intrigued when I arrived at the address to hear loud rock-and-roll music blasting from inside a house whose grass was higher than the broken white picket fence that surrounded the front yard. As I walked up the walk toward the front door, I noticed that the shutters were crooked, several panes of glass were missing from the windows and the front door was off its hinges.

As I entered the house, I saw a javelin sticking through the living room wall, a group of people bowling down the hallway and a packed dance floor with a lot of cute girls. As I made my way through the house, one of the fraternity members came up and introduced himself. He saw my nametag and asked if my father had flown U-2s. Instantly, I thought that it was going to be like high school all over again. Fortunately, I was wrong. The guy who asked, Jay Rose, was an exceptionally good friend who was a groomsman in my wedding.

As a result of joining the fraternity, I came out of my shell, I started to comb my hair in a unique way, I started to become more self-confident. I moved into the fraternity house and took on a leadership role with the fraternity and eventually was elected chapter president. While at CSUN, I was able to participate and excelled in several intramural sports. Best of all, I became more comfortable around girls and enjoyed going out on dates. As my self-confidence grew, my grades slid. I was working part time, partying full time and sleeping through classes. It was no surprise that I received a letter from the dean saying that due to my declining grades I should take some time to evaluate what I wanted to do with my life.

Having just chaired the twenty-fifth anniversary reunion for the fraternity and realizing that I was not going to be allowed to attend classes the following semester, I called one of the alumni I had met at the reunion, Vance T. Meyers, who was the vice president for Pardee Construction, a Weyerhaeuser subsidiary, and told him of my interest in working in the construction industry. The interview went well, and I was hired to work in the human resources department. I worked there for two years and during that time moved to a small basement apartment in Hollywood Hills. One day I noticed that a position had opened up in the land acquisition department. I applied, interviewed and was told that my construction experience was good, my performance at Pardee was good, but I lacked a college degree, so they could not hire me. Within a week, I had enrolled at California State University, Los Angeles, and while working full time at Pardee Construction earned my bachelor's degree in philosophy.

Upon graduating, I quit Pardee Construction and moved with a friend up to Mammoth Lakes, California. I got a job working construction by day and as a night auditor for the local hotel, which earned me a free ski pass. I was in heaven. I skied every day in the winter, hiked and biked every day in the summer.

About one year and a half after I had moved to Mammoth Mountain, I received word from a cousin that my father's mother, grandmother Ida, had passed away on the family farm in Pound, Virginia. I made arrangements to attend the funeral and realized during the services that I did not know my family that well and that it had been ten years since I had seen them. It was then that I decided to move to Virginia in order to get to know my family better and also further my education.

Within six months of my return to California, I had sold everything I could, including my car and stereo equipment; bought a one-way plane ticket for Dulles Airport; and in July 1992 moved to Northern Virginia. The first few weeks in Virginia, I lived with an aunt and uncle in Falls Church before renting a room in a townhouse in the city of Fairfax, Virginia.

Between the years 1992 and 1995, I attended George Mason University, worked part time for the GMU Department of Public and International Affairs and also part time for the City of Fairfax as Assistant Registrar. In 1995, I graduated with my master's degree in public administration (MPA) and also earned a certificate of nonprofit management.

In 1996, while working for the Downtown Fairfax Coalition, a small nonprofit dedicated to the historical revitalization of Old Town Fairfax, I met my future wife, Miss Jennifer Webber, at the annual Festival of Lights and Carols. After a five-year courtship, we married on May 28, 2000; bought a house; and started to settle down.

On July 1, 1996, I founded The Cold War Museum (www.coldwar.org) to honor Cold War veterans and preserve Cold War history. Currently, a mobile exhibit travels internationally, displaying historical artifacts associated with the U-2 Incident of May 1960. The traveling exhibit promotes The Cold War Museum, which exhibits artifacts and memorabilia associated with various Cold War events from the end of World War II to the collapse of the Soviet Union. In conjunction with the museum, a "Cold War Memorial" will eventually honor the men and women who worked toward the preservation of democracy during the Cold War from 1945 to 1991.

In addition to working full time and volunteering for The Cold War Museum Board of Directors, I also took it on myself in 1996 to start writing letters to the U.S. Air Force, CIA and other government agencies requesting that my father's military records be updated so that he would be eligible for the Prisoner of War Medal because of his twenty-one months' incarceration in the former Soviet Union.

At the same time, I also started writing letters to the U.S. Air Force to request a flight on a U-2 so that I could experience something that would bring me closer to my father. As the fortieth anniversary of my father's shoot down neared, I received a telephone call from a good friend, Buzz Carpenter, a former SR-71 pilot who at the time was working for Raytheon E Systems. He informed me that several colleagues were able to work out the details so that Dad would be honored with the POW Medal, and I would be authorized to take a flight on the U-2. It was coordinated as a way to promote the U-2 program and help recruit new pilots.

A few days before May 1, 2000, I arrived at Beale Air Force Base in California. There I was briefed, suited up into a flight pressure suit and trained on emergency escape from the U-2.

About 10:00 a.m. PST I climbed into a U-2R aircraft piloted by Major Brian Anderson. After a long takeoff run, we were aloft. Forty years after my father's infamous flight into Soviet airspace, I was flying in a U-2 above the United States. The flight was the thrill of a lifetime. I flew for about three hours over California. I reached an altitude of 73,130 feet and was able to see the curvature of the Earth. It was incredible.

Upon landing, I was escorted to the reviewing stands, where my mother, sister and wife were waiting. Once we were seated, Base Commander General Chilton posthumously presented the Distinguished Flying Cross, Prisoner of War Medal and National Service Medal to the family. In addition, CIA representative Joan Dempsey presented the CIA's Director's Medal to the family. This was an unexpected bonus, which the family deeply appreciated.

The posthumous presentation of my father's medals by the U.S. Air Force and the CIA on May 1, 2000, helped to close the chapter on the U-2 Incident. The Powers family is deeply appreciative to the U.S. Air Force, CIA and many others for their help in the May 1, 2000 U-2 flight and medal presentation. For the Powers family, it was long overdue, but it goes to show that it is never too late to set the record straight.

12

NOTABLE COLD WAR VIRGINIANS

SENATOR JOHN WARNER

John Warner was elected to the U.S. Senate in 1978 and served five consecutive terms, establishing a record as the second-longest-serving U.S. senator in Virginia's history. He served on the Senate Armed Services Committee, holding positions as chairman or ranking member for his last seventeen years. A decorated Cold War and Korean War veteran, Warner volunteered for active military duty as an enlisted sailor in the final years of World War II from 1945 to 1946. He was seventeen years old when he entered military service.[119] Several years later, he enlisted in the U.S. Marines and served as a commissioned officer, first lieutenant, in the Korean War from 1950 to 1952.

He graduated from the University of Virginia School of Law in 1953, and from 1955 to 1960, he was an assistant U.S. attorney for the District of Columbia. He joined Hogan & Hartson (now Hogan Lovell's) as an associate in 1961, became a partner in 1964, departed in 1968 for a career in public service and rejoined in 2009. In 1969, he was nominated by President Richard Nixon, and confirmed by the Senate, as undersecretary, and later as secretary, of the U.S. Navy, serving from 1969 to 1974 during the Vietnam War.

As secretary, Warner negotiated the Incidents at Sea Agreement with the Soviet Union in 1972.[120] The agreement was precipitated to avoid further incidents of American and Soviet ships bumping into each other and both ships and aircraft making threatening movements against those of the other side, among other tenets. The agreement was countersigned by Soviet Admiral Sergei Gorshkov during the Moscow summit meeting in 1972.

For a time, Warner may have been best known nationally as the dashing sixth husband of the actress Elizabeth Taylor. Her celebrity was a draw on the campaign trail during his difficult first race for the Senate in 1978, an election he won narrowly to start his political career. The couple divorced in 1982.[121]

JOHN O. MARSH

Born in Winchester, Virginia, in 1926, Marsh enlisted in the Army as a private in 1944. Two years later, he was commissioned as a second lieutenant at age nineteen, serving with U.S. occupation forces in Germany for two years. Marsh went on to serve in both the Army Reserve and the National Guard, retiring in 1976 at the rank of lieutenant colonel.[122]

Marsh started his political career as a Democratic congressman from Virginia, serving four terms from 1963 to 1971, changing political parties and declining to seek reelection in 1970. Marsh went on to serve in a series of positions in the Nixon and Ford administrations, coming to be regarded as one of President Gerald Ford's most effective and influential aides.

Marsh returned to private law practice until Ronald Reagan won the presidency in 1980. Soon after his inauguration, Reagan named Marsh secretary of the Army in January 1981. As secretary, Marsh presided over the rebuilding of the Army, winning increases for the Army budget by 30 percent and throwing his support behind the enhancement of special operations forces in the wake of the 1979 "Desert One" fiasco, the failed rescue attempt of Americans held hostage in Iran.

Marsh was personally involved in persuading Congress to support the deployment of the Pershing II missile system to Germany. The Pershing II deployment is usually cited as the primary reason the Soviet Union agreed to the Intermediate-Range Nuclear Forces (INF) Treaty. It is no small exaggeration to say that because of Marsh's efforts, the Army was able to defeat Saddam Hussein's armed forces in one hundred hours in 1991 in Desert Storm. Eventually, Marsh became the longest-serving secretary of the Army in its nearly 250-year history, serving 8 years and 6 months.[122]

SENATOR JIM WEBB

The son of a career pilot in the U.S. Air Force, Jim Webb enrolled in the U.S. Naval Academy, graduating in 1968. After graduating first in his class at the Marine Corps Officer's Basic School, Webb deployed to Vietnam to serve as rifle platoon and company commander of Delta Company, First Battalion, Fifth Marine Regiment, during a period when the number of U.S. personnel killed in action averaged more than four hundred per week. During his tour of Vietnam, Webb was awarded the Navy Cross and two Purple Hearts. His injuries ended his active-duty career in 1972. One of his Purple Hearts awarded read: "First Lieutenant James H. Webb, Jr. United States Marine Corps, for extraordinary heroism while serving as a Platoon Commander with Company D, First Battalion, Fifth Marines, FIRST Marine Division (Reinforced), Fleet Marine Force, in connection with combat operations against the enemy in the Republic of Vietnam on July 10, 1969."[123]

After graduating from the Georgetown University Law Center in 1975, Webb embarked on a career in government with a focus on veterans' affairs and armed forces modernization. He served as minority counsel for the House Committee on Veterans Affairs, assistant secretary of defense for Reserve Affairs, secretary of the Navy and U.S. senator from Virginia from 2007 to 2013. Webb was the first Naval Academy graduate to serve in the military and then become secretary of the Navy. As senator, Webb drafted, introduced and built bipartisan support in both the House and Senate to pass the "post-9/11 GI Bill," which was signed into law in 2008.

A fellow of the Harvard University Institute of Politics, Webb has received more than twenty national awards for his public service, including the Thomas Jefferson Foundation Medal (the University of Virginia's highest external honor), the American Legion Public Service Award and the Congressional Medal of Honor Society Patriot Award.

In addition to his public service, Webb has enjoyed a storied career as a writer. His commentaries on national security, foreign relations and domestic issues have been published in a wide range of major magazines and newspapers. Traveling widely as a journalist, he received an Emmy Award for his PBS coverage of the U.S. Marines in Beirut in 1983 and in 2004 was embedded with the U.S. military in Afghanistan. He authored the original story and was executive producer of the film *Rules of Engagement*, which held the top slot in U.S. box offices for two weeks in April 2000.[124]

SENATOR CHUCK ROBB

In 1961, well before anti–Vietnam War fervor seared Madison, Wisconsin, Charles Robb was often seen walking down Langdon Street in his ROTC drill uniform on his way to his Chi Phi fraternity.[125] He was brigade commander of all campus ROTC units and went on to a Marine Corps career that led to his being stationed at the White House as a social aide. There, he met President Lyndon Johnson's daughter Lynda Bird Johnson, and the two were married in an elegant 1967 White House wedding.

But Robb did not hide behind prominent connections. He served two infantry combat tours in Vietnam and was awarded the Bronze Star. After his military career, he earned a law degree at the University of Virginia and went on to serve decades in public life. During the 1960s, he served on active duty with the United States Marine Corps, retiring from the Marine Corps Reserve in 1991.

Robb began as the class honor graduate from Marine Officer's Basic School in 1961 and ended up as head of the principal recruiting program for Marine officers in 1970. In between, he served in both the 1st and 2nd Marine Divisions, and his assignments included duty as a military social aide at the White House and command of an infantry company in combat in Vietnam.[126]

The Democrat rose from Virginia's lieutenant governor to its governor in 1982, and after serving a single term, he was overwhelmingly elected to the U.S. Senate. Robb served as lieutenant governor of Virginia from 1978 to 1982, as governor of Virginia from 1982 to 1986 and then as a U.S. senator from 1989 until 2001.[127]

13

DOOMSDAY PLANNING FOR THE THIRD WORLD WAR

Plans for a Third World War were well underway as the two superpowers of the United States and the Soviet Union became the dominant countries in the West and East, respectively. After the Soviet Union tested its own atomic bomb in 1949, followed by the fall of China to the Communists, these and other events heightened further tensions that world war would become a possibility. As the Cold War continued in earnest, procedures to keep the government functioning in the United States were deemed essential for war planning.

Primary sites built to continue the federal government functioning during a possible Third World War were located in Virginia, West Virginia, Pennsylvania, Maryland and Washington, D.C. For purposes of this text, the sites in Virginia and across the border into the Allegheny Mountains in West Virginia are mentioned in detail. There were also regional sites of note in Maryland, Pennsylvania and Washington, D.C., that acted in this communication system. It was these sites that housed communications and living quarters for the White House, Congress, Federal Reserve and other governmental bodies to function through the aftermath of a nuclear war. What was missing from all of these plans was how various officials would make it to these sprawling sites, given the variables of highway, rail or air traffic being operable in time of war.

Audio Visual Conservation Center, Culpeper, Virginia. *Library of Congress, Packard Center.*

CULPEPER SWITCH: KEEP THE CHECKS ROLLING

Named the Culpeper Switch, this sprawling underground facility was constructed in the town of Culpeper, Virginia, in 1969. The purpose of this underground bunker was to house both Federal Reserve employees and vast amounts of money to the tune of $4 billion in order to restart the economy after the nuclear fallout. The building is a 140,000-square-foot hardened underground complex built by the U.S. Treasury Department and the Federal Reserve, completed in 1969.

Until 1988, several billion dollars in currency was stored there to resupply the nation in the event of a devastating nuclear attack.[128]

PRESIDENTIAL EMERGENCY FACILITY SITES

Mount Weather (Crystal), Berryville, Virginia, and Martinsburg
(Cowpuncher) and Roundtop Summit, Virginia

North Mountain is a mountain ridge within the Ridge-and-Valley Appalachians in the state of West Virginia. The span consists of twenty miles of ridge line and is noticeably higher in elevation, containing the mountain's highest point of 1,673 feet above sea level at its Round Top summit near Arden in Berkeley County, West Virginia. North Mountain's Roundtop Summit is also the site of a deactivated microwave relay station that was used during the Cold War.

Roundtop Summit, built in the late 1950s and early 1960s, was located on North Mountain and west of Arden, West Virginia. Its proximity to

Washington, D.C., and these other key locations made it a prime choice for a microwave relay station during the Cold War.

Construction of Cowpuncher tower was completed during the late '50s and early '60s. Originally named Copper, the cylindrical tower was renamed Cowpuncher in 1965. Cowpuncher was exactly the same construction and served the same purpose as Cannonball Relay in Mercersburg, Pennsylvania. The tower was part of a microwave network designed to provide communications to the president of the United States and emergency communications in the event of a nuclear attack. The microwave route connected Camp David, Mount Weather, Site R and other key bodies of government directly to the White House. Not only would the microwave network provide reliable communications, but the various sites also could serve as relocation facilities to withstand a nuclear attack.

From these sites, the president could communicate with and address the American people.

Each facility had equipment to carry voice, video and secure voice and teletype. Of course, with our cellular networks today, such facilities are no longer necessary, and even private citizens can communicate as long as the cellular towers still function.

There were seven facilities in the Presidential Emergency Network, each operated by the White House Communications Agency. Manned switchboards and communication centers were at each terminal. These communications centers became active in the event of a national emergency. The facility was deactivated in 1970 and closed in 1977, with the tower being demolished around 1983.

The full list of sites were

Site 1. Cactus Terminal, Camp David, Thurmont, Maryland
Site 2. Cannonball Relay, Mercersburg, Pennsylvania
Site 3. Cowpuncher Relay, Martinsburg, West Virginia
Site 4. Cartwheel Terminal, Washington, D.C.
Site 5. Crystal Terminal, Mount Weather, Virginia
Site 6. Cadre (or Creed) Terminal, aka Site R, Blue Ridge Summit, Pennsylvania
Site 7. Corkscrew Relay, Boonsboro, Maryland
Final Destination. Crown, the White House, Washington, D.C.

TOWER HISTORY AND PURPOSE

The famous Mount Weather Special Facility, a federal continuity of government installation and a presidential relocation site, featured a White House Communications Agency (WHCA) switchboard and communication center and two hardened microwave towers linking it to the other White House emergency sites. This facility also interfaced directly with the Civil Defense Emergency Broadcast System (EBS) located at Mount Weather allowing video interface with the WHCA microwave network.

These cylindrical concrete towers were similar in design to the Cannonball facility but were almost completely underground except for the Plexiglas-covered antenna decks that composed the two uppermost levels of the towers. The towers were connected by tunnels to Mount Weather's main underground complex.

The Crystal towers are located on the east and west sides of Mount Weather; the east tower's microwave link connected to the Cartwheel facility, and the west tower's microwave link communicated with Cowpuncher, located on Roundtop Mountain west of Martinsburg, West Virginia. Cowpuncher was identical to the Cannonball tower, but it has been demolished and no evidence of it remains at the site.[129]

GREENBRIER HOTEL, WEST VIRGINIA

In the late 1950s, the U.S. government approached the Greenbrier resort and sought its assistance in creating a secret emergency relocation center to house Congress due to the Cuban revolution and soon after the Cuban Missile Crisis. The classified underground facility was built at the same time as the West Virginia Wing, an aboveground addition to the hotel, from 1959 to 1962. For thirty years, the Greenbrier owners maintained an agreement with the federal government that, in the event of an international crisis, the entire resort property would be converted to government use, specifically as the emergency location for the legislative branch.

Eisenhower decided the Greenbrier would be a perfect cover for a congressional bunker. In 1958, government workers broke ground on what they called "Project Greek Island." It was just about a four-hour drive from Washington. Hotel workers and guests were told that the giant hole in the ground would house a new conference facility. Technically that was correct, but this new construction would be accessible to only a few.

Top: Greenbrier Hotel. *Library of Congress*.

Bottom: Greenbrier Hotel hallway. *Library of Congress*.

Finally, there was a mysterious crew of TV technicians who worked at the hotel but did not work for the hotel. The company they worked for was called Forsyth Associates. As it turned out, Forsyth Associates was a cover: these were secret government employees who had to keep the bunker in a constant state of operational readiness.

"For those 30 years, you had to make sure all the filters were changed, all the pharmaceuticals were up-to-date, and all the food was ready to go," Bob Conte said. That would be a six-month supply of food, periodically refreshed.[130]

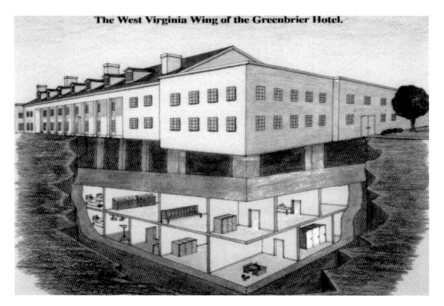

Greenbrier Hotel Doomsday Bunker depiction for members of Congress. *Library of Congress.*

The project used a cut-and-cover style construction method for the creation of the bunker, where material, known as spoil, is removed from the surface and carried away from the site to create a space in which the bunker is constructed. In the case of the Project Greek Island Bunker, the spoil was used in the expansion of a nine-hole golf course and as fill material in a runway extension project at the local municipal airfield. This prevented detection of the project.

The underground facility contained a dormitory, kitchen, hospital and broadcast center for members of Congress. The broadcast center had changeable seasonal backdrops to allow it to appear as if members of Congress were broadcasting from Washington, D.C. A 100-foot radio tower was installed 4.5 miles away for these broadcasts. The largest room is the Exhibit Hall, 89 by 186 feet beneath a ceiling nearly 20 feet high and supported by 18 support columns.

Adjoining it are two smaller auditoriums, one seating about 470 people, big enough to host the 435-member House of Representatives, and the smaller with a seating capacity of about 130, suitable as a temporary Senate chamber. The Exhibit Hall itself could be used for joint sessions of Congress. What was used by Greenbrier guests for business meetings was actually a disguised work area for members of Congress, complete with four hidden blast doors. Two of the doors were large enough to allow vehicles to enter.

One weighed more than twenty-eight short tons and measured twelve feet, three inches wide and fifteen feet high. Another weighed more than twenty short tons. The doors were nineteen and a half inches thick. The two-foot-thick walls of the bunker were made of reinforced concrete designed to withstand a nearby nuclear blast.

Kate's Mountain linked the secret congressional relocation facility at the nearby Greenbrier resort hotel to the AT&T Long Lines microwave network. An underground cable connected the two sites.[131]

INTERIOR DEPARTMENT BOMB SHELTER, HARPERS FERRY, WEST VIRGINIA

A bomb shelter is located under the lawn north of the National Park Service's Stephen P. Mather Training Center, formerly Storer College, off Fillmore Street in Harpers Ferry, West Virginia. The history of the shelter is still being investigated, but available information indicates that it was an emergency relocation site for the Department of the Interior headquarters and the secretary of the interior.

Personnel access to the shelter is through a metal door, apparently of standard commercial design, set into a retaining wall adjacent to the driveway serving the Training Center's parking lot. There is no vehicular entrance to the shelter, only a parking space in front of the entrance.

The space is now used by the NPS Interpretive Design Center.[132]

MOUNT WEATHER, BERRYVILLE, VIRGINIA

The Mount Weather Special Facility is a continuity of government facility operated by the Federal Emergency Management Agency (FEMA). The 200,000-square-foot facility also houses FEMA's National Emergency Coordinating Center. Located on a 434-acre mountain site on the borders of Loudoun and Clarke Counties, the aboveground support facilities include about a dozen buildings providing communications links to the White House Situation Room.

In 1954, a few high-level officials, assuming several hours' warning of a hypothetical attack, left Washington with a checklist of possible actions.

They assembled in a cave and found that water was dripping from the ceiling and from the walls. This was the setting for the first Operation Alert exercise. The exercise lasted only a few hours, but a great deal was learned.

As of July 1958, there were some ninety relocation sites in the seat of government arc from thirty to three hundred miles of Washington and over three hundred relocation sites throughout the country for regional and field offices. The arc was connected with an interagency communication system, which was reasonably adequate and was in the process of further development. A few highly secure relocation sites for central direction and for the protection of central communications had either been constructed or were under construction as of mid-1958.

The Army Corps of Engineers completed the "Area B" underground complex in 1958–59. Total construction costs, adjusted for inflation, are estimated to have exceeded $1 billion. The entrance is protected by a guillotine gate and a ten-foot-tall by twenty-foot-wide thirty-four-ton blast door that is five feet thick and reportedly takes ten to fifteen minutes to open or close.

The underground bunker includes a hospital, a crematorium, dining and recreation areas, sleeping quarters, reservoirs of drinking and cooling water, an emergency power plant and a radio and television studio that is part of the Emergency Broadcasting System. A series of side tunnels accommodate a total of twenty office buildings, some of which are three stories tall.

An on-site 90,000 gallon/day sewage treatment plant and two 250,000-gallon aboveground storage tanks are intended to support a population of two hundred for up to thirty days. Although the facility is designed to accommodate several thousand people (with sleeping cots for two thousand), only the president, the cabinet and Supreme Court were provided private sleeping quarters. For continuity of government purposes, senior officials are divided into Alpha, Bravo and Charlie teams—the first remains in Washington, the second relocates to Mount Weather and the third disperses to other relocation sites.

The complex was prepared to assume certain governmental powers at the time of the 1961 Cuban Missile Crisis and the assassination of President Kennedy in 1963. The first full-scale activation of the facility came on November 9, 1965, at the time of the great northeastern power blackout. The installation used the tools of its Civil Crisis Management program on a standby basis during the 1967 and 1968 urban riots and during a number of national antiwar demonstrations.

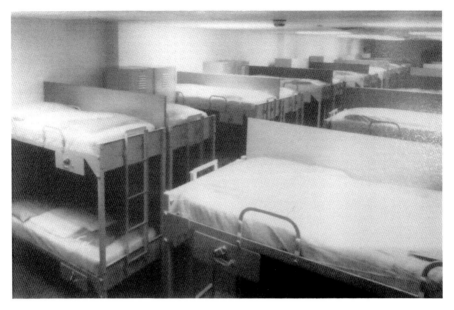

Bunk beds in the underground bunker at the Greenbrier Hotel. *Library of Congress.*

On December 1, 1974, a TWA Boeing 727 jet crashed into a fog-wrapped mountain, killing all ninety-two persons aboard. Journalists who covered the crash site noticed a fenced U.S. government facility nearby. Within days, the *Washington Post* reported that the facility was known as Mount Weather, though the *Post* quoted a spokesman for the Department of Defense as saying he was not allowed "to comment on what Mt. Weather was used for…or how long it has been in its current use."[133]

• • • •

Visit The Cold War Museum's website at www.coldwar.org
for more information about this fascinating era of history.

NOTES

1. Project Nike in Virginia: Defending Cold War Skies

1. The Military Standard, "Nike Missile Locations in Virginia," http://www.themilitarystandard.com/missile/nike/locationsvi.php.

2. The Cold War and the Race to Space

2. Christopher Sturdevant, *Cold War Wisconsin* (Charleston, SC: The History Press, 2018), 48–51.
3. NASA, "NACA Overview," https://history.nasa.gov/naca/overview.html.
4. James Schefter, *The Race: The Uncensored Story of How America Beat Russia to the Moon* (New York: Doubleday, 1999).
5. Royal Museums Greenwich, "Space Race Timeline," https://www.rmg.co.uk/stories/topics/space-race-timeline.
6. NASA Space Science Data Coordinated Archive [hereafter NSSDC], "Mercury Redstone 3," https://nssdc.gsfc.nasa.gov/nmc/spacecraft/display.action?id=MERCR3.
7. Paul Dickson, *Dictionary of the Space Age* (Baltimore, MD: Johns Hopkins University Press, 2009).
8. NSSDC, "Gemini 3," https://nssdc.gsfc.nasa.gov/nmc/spacecraft/display.action?id=1965-024A.

9. NSSDC, "The Apollo Program (1963–1972)," https://nssdc.gsfc.nasa. gov/planetary/lunar/apollo.html.

10. NSSDC, "Apollo 7," https://nssdc.gsfc.nasa.gov/nmc/spacecraft/ display.action?id=1968-089A.

11. NASA, "50 Years Ago: Launch of Salyut, the World's First Space Station," https://www.nasa.gov/missions/station/50-years-ago-launch-of-salyut-the-worlds-first-space-station/.

12. NASA, "Langley 100: A Storied Legacy, a Soaring Future," https:// www.nasa.gov/centers-and-facilities/langley/nasalangley100-a-storied-legacy-a-soaring-future/.

13. Stephen Garber and Roger Launius, "A Brief History of the National Aeronautics and Space Administration," https://history.nasa.gov/SP-4225/documentation/brief-history/history.htm.

3. The National Reconnaissance Office and Evolution of Satellites

14. Bruce Berkowitz, *The National Reconnaissance Office at 50 Years: A Brief History* (Chantilly, VA: National Reconnaissance Office, 2011), https:// www.nro.gov/Portals/65/documents/history/csnr/programs/NRO_ Brief_History.pdf.

15. James Bamford, "Clandestine Air War: The Truth Behind Cold War US Surveillance Flights," *Harvard International Review* 23, no. 4 (Winter 2002): 86–88.

16. Internet Archive WayBack Machine, "LMSD Satellite Systems Briefing, Part II: The Samos Program September 14, 1959," https:// web.archive.org/web/20130224040132/http://www.nro.gov/foia/ declass/WS117L_Records/670.PDF.

17. Peter Suciu, "The Top-Secret Eye in the Sky: The History of the HEXAGON KH-9 Photo Reconnaissance Satellite," Clearance Jobs, June 3, 2019, https://news.clearancejobs.com/2019/06/03/ the-top-secret-eye-in-the-sky-the-history-of-the-hexagon-kh-9-photo-reconnaissance-satellite/.

18. National Reconnaissance Office, declassified documents, Project Gambit, http://nro.gov/foia/declass/GAMHEX/GAMBIT/2.PDF.

4. Virginia Military Bases During the Cold War

19. Official United States Marine Corps, "Crossroads of the Marine Corps," https://www.quantico.marines.mil/Home/About/.
20. Cheryl Johnson, interviews with the authors.
21. Charles Butler, "Naval Cold War Architecture in the Cold War Era," Virginia Department of Historic Resources, https://www.dhr.virginia.gov/pdf_files/newdominion/Naval%20Cold%20War%20Architecture_TButler_final.pdf.
22. U.S. Fleet Forces Command, "A Long, Distinguished History," https://www.usff.navy.mil/About-Us/History/.
23. Nicola Davis, "Soviet Submarine Officer Who Averted Nuclear War Honored with Prize," *Guardian*, October 27, 2017, https://www.theguardian.com/science/2017/oct/27/vasili-arkhipov-soviet-submarine-captain-who-averted-nuclear-war-awarded-future-of-life-prize.
24. Commander, Navy Region Southeast, "Strategic Weapons Facility, Atlantic," https://cnrse.cnic.navy.mil/Installations/SUBASE-Kings-Bay/About/Tenant-Commands/Strategic-Weapons-Facility-Atlantic/.
25. Encyclopedia Virginia, "Naval Station Norfolk," https://encyclopediavirginia.org/entries/naval-station-norfolk/.
26. John Mintz, "Nitro Blast Rocks Army Munitions Plant," *Washington Post*, February 7, 1985, https://www.washingtonpost.com/archive/local/1985/02/07/nitro-blast-rocks-army-munitions-plant/85be0e3d-aae3-4a01-be7d-946fe5db5d5c/.
27. Radford Army Ammunition Plant, Installation Restoration Program, "Location and History," https://www.radfordaapirp.org/about/history.htm.
28. Joint Base Langley-Eustis, "Langley Air Force Base History," https://www.jble.af.mil/About-Us/633rd-Air-Base-Wing-History/.
29. Navy Region Mid-Atlantic, "History of Naval Weapons Station Yorktown," https://cnrma.cnic.navy.mil/Installations/WPNSTA-Yorktown/About/History/.
30. Military Bases, "Warrenton Training Center Army Base in Alexandria, VA," https://militarybases.com/virginia/warrenton-training-center/.
31. Military Standard, "Nike Missile Locations in Virginia."
32. Department of the Air Force Unit Histories, "22nd AIR DEFENSE MISSILE SQUADRON (BOMARC)," https://usafunithistory.com/PDF/20-29/22%20AIR%20DEFENSE%20MISSILE%20SQ.pdf.

33. James Olson, "The Nuclear Superhighway," *True Spies*, episode 21, https://spyscape.com/podcast/the-nuclear-superhighway.
34. Stephanie Hubka, "Vint Hill Farms Station: Cold War History in DC's Backyard," Road Unraveled, June 6, 2019, https://www.roadunraveled.com/blog/vint-hill-farms-station/.
35. John Salmon, "Vint Hill Farms Station Historic District Significance Statement," prepared at the request and on behalf of Citizens for Fauquier County 'CFFC,'" 2014, http://vinthilllofts.com/history/.
36. Claudette Roulo, "10 Things You Probably Didn't Know About the Pentagon," DOD News, January 3, 2019, https://www.defense.gov/News/Feature-Stories/story/Article/1650913/10-things-you-probably-didnt-know-about-the-pentagon/.
37. Katie Lange, "Pentagon History: 7 Big Things to Know," DOD News, December 19, 2019, https://www.defense.gov/News/Feature-Stories/story/Article/1867440/pentagon-history-7-big-things-to-know/.
38. George Bergstrom, "The Pentagon. Washington, D.C., United States of America," Architectuul, https://architectuul.com/architecture/the-pentagon.

5. Woodrow Wilson and the Origins of the Cold War

39. Britannica, "First Term as President of Woodrow Wilson," https://www.britannica.com/biography/Woodrow-Wilson/First-term-as-president.
40. National Archives, "16th Amendment to the U.S. Constitution: Federal Income Tax (1913)," https://www.archives.gov/milestone-documents/16th-amendment.
41. National Archives, "17th Amendment to the U.S. Constitution: Direct Election of U.S. Senators (1913)," https://www.archives.gov/milestone-documents/17th-amendment.
42. National Constitution Center, "Espionage Act of 1917 and Sedition Act of 1918 (1917–1918)," https://constitutioncenter.org/the-constitution/historic-document-library/detail/espionage-act-of-1917-and-sedition-act-of-1918-1917-1918.
43. Tim Weiner, *Enemies: A History of the FBI* (New York: Random House, 2012).
44. Steven Parfitt, "The Justice Department Campaign against the IWW, 1917–1920," IWW History Project, https://depts.washington.edu/iww/justice_dept.shtml.

45. Herbert Hoover Presidential Library and Museum, "Years of Compassion 1914–1923," https://hoover.archives.gov/exhibits/years-compassion-1914-1923.

46. Benjamin Weissman, "Herbert Hoover and Famine Relief to Soviet Russia, 1921–1923," Hoover Institution, https://www.hoover.org/research/herbert-hoover-and-famine-relief-soviet-russia-1921-1923.

47. Britannica, "Fourteen Points, United States Declaration," https://www.britannica.com/event/Fourteen-Points.

48. Office of the Historian, "The League of Nations, 1920," *Milestones: 1914–1920*, https://history.state.gov/milestones/1914-1920/league.

49. Sturdevant, *Cold War Wisconsin*, 17–24.

6. Atoms for Peace: Atomic Energy for Mankind

50. Dwight D. Eisenhower Presidential Library, Museum & Boyhood Home, "Atoms for Peace," https://www.eisenhowerlibrary.gov/research/online-documents/atoms-peace.

51. International Atomic Energy Agency, "Atoms for Peace Speech," https://www.iaea.org/about/history/atoms-for-peace-speech.

52. Library of Congress, "1-21 Ship Stabilization System—Nuclear Ship Savannah, Various Ports Operated by the U.S. Maritime Administration, Washington, District of Columbia, DC Drawings from Survey HAER DC-64," https://www.loc.gov/resource/hhh.dc1047.sheet/?sp=21.

53. MuseumShips, "NS Savannah," https://museumships.us/merchantmarine/savannah.

54. Radiationworks, "NS Otto Hahn—Germany's Nuclear Powered Cargo Ship," https://www.radiationworks.com/ships/nsottohahn.htm.

55. Internet Archive WayBack Machine, "Atoms for Peace Award, Inc. Records, 1944–1972. Institute Archives and Special Collections. Processed: December 1984 by Elizabeth Craig-McCormack," https://web.archive.org/web/20100311073706/http://libraries.mit.edu/archives/research/collections/collections-mc/pdf/mc10.pdf.

56. Bulletin of the Atomic Scientists, "'Atoms for Peace,' Cancer Research and Nuclear Energy in a Postwar America," https://thebulletin.org/virtual-tour/atoms-for-peace-cancer-research-and-nuclear-energy-in-a-postwar-america/.

57. Argonne National Laboratory, "Our History: Inspiring the Nation's Future," https://www.anl.gov/our-history.

58. Ariana Rowberry, "Sixty Years of 'Atoms for Peace' and Iran's Nuclear Program," Brookings, December 18, 2013, https://www.brookings.edu/articles/sixty-years-of-atoms-for-peace-and-irans-nuclear-program/.
59. Atomic Gardens, an Online History, "Born from the Bomb," https://www.atomicgardening.com/1945/08/09/nagasaki-plant-mutations/.
60. Arul Suresh, "Atoms in the Garden," Stanford University, 2017, http://large.stanford.edu/courses/2017/ph241/suresh2/.
61. Ripley's, "Atomic Gardening in the 1950s," https://www.ripleys.com/weird-news/atomic-gardening/.
62. James Wong, "Gardens: Expose Yourself to Atomic Gardening," March 13, 2016, https://www.theguardian.com/lifeandstyle/2016/mar/13/growing-atomically-energised-plants-james-wong.
63. Lawrence Livermore National Library, "The Plowshare Program," https://st.llnl.gov/news/look-back/plowshare-program.

7. Creation of the Central Intelligence Agency

64. Bible Gateway, https://www.biblegateway.com/passage/?search=Numbers+13&version=GW.
65. National Park Service, "'Wild Bill' Donovan and the Origins of the OSS," https://www.nps.gov/articles/wild-bill-donovan-and-the-origins-of-the-oss.htm.
66. National Park Service, "William 'Wild Bill' Donovan," https://www.nps.gov/people/william-wild-bill-donovan.htm.
67. Central Intelligence Agency [hereafter CIA], "Cloak and Dagger: The Unexpected Beginnings of CIA," https://www.cia.gov/stories/story/cloak-and-dagger-the-unexpected-beginnings-of-cia/.
68. CIA, "About CIA—Organization," https://www.cia.gov/about/organization/.
69. Sig Mickelson, *America's Other Voice: The Story of Radio Free Europe and Radio Liberty* (New York: Praeger, 1983).
70. Dwight Schear, "Berlin Bell's Toll Heard by World," Stars and Stripes, October 25, 1950, https://www.stripes.com/news/berlin-bell-s-toll-heard-by-world-1.78164.
71. Christopher Simpson, *Blowback: America's Recruitment of Nazis and Its Effects on the Cold War* (New York: Weidenfeld & Nicolson, 1988).

72. Serge Schmemann, "Soviet Union Ends Years of Jamming of Radio Liberty," *New York Times*, December 1, 1988, https://www.nytimes.com/1988/12/01/world/soviet-union-ends-years-of-jamming-of-radio-liberty.html.

73. David P. Hadley, *The Rising Clamor: The American Press, the Central Intelligence Agency, and the Cold War* (Lexington: University Press of Kentucky, 2019).

74. As told through interviews with George Georgieff's granddaughter Jill Fuller.

75. CIA, "MEMORANDUM FOR: Chief, Fl SUBJECT: Project AEDEPOT Renewal," https://www.cia.gov/readingroom/docs/AEDEPOT%20%20%20VOL.%201_0016.pdf.

76. Fabian Escalante, *Executive Action: 634 Ways to Kill Fidel Castro* (Melbourne: Ocean Press, 2006).

77. Glenn Kessler, "Trying to Kill Fidel Castro," *Washington Post*, June 27, 2007.

78. Thomas Maier, *Mafia Spies: The Inside Story of the CIA, Gangsters, JFK, and Castro* (New York: Skyhorse Publishing, 2019).

79. Del Hahn, *Smuggler's End: The Life and Death of Barry Seal* (Gretna, LA: Pelican Publishing, 2016); *The Invisible Pilot*, TV miniseries, HBO, 2022.

80. "IN SUMMARY; Nicaragua Downs Plane and Survivor Implicates C.I.A.," *New York Times*, October 12, 1986, https://www.nytimes.com/1986/10/12/weekinreview/in-summary-nicaragua-downs-plane-and-survivor-implicates-cia.html.

81. CIA Museum, https://www.cia.gov/legacy/museum/.

82. CIA, "Honoring Our Fallen Officers," May 23, 2017, https://www.cia.gov/stories/story/honoring-our-fallen/.

83. CIA Memorial Wall, https://intelligence.fandom.com/wiki/CIA_Memorial_Wall.

84. Ibid.

8. The Federal Bureau of Investigation: Fighting Enemies Within

85. FBI, "What Is the Mission of the FBI?" https://www.fbi.gov/about/faqs/what-is-the-mission-of-the-fbi.

86. FBI, "What Is the FBI?" https://www.fbi.gov/about/faqs/what-is-the-fbi.

87. Biography, "J. Edgar Hoover," https://www.biography.com/legal-figures/j-edgar-hoover.

88. Christopher Sturdevant, *Cold War Illinois* (Charleston, SC: The History Press, 2020), 28–29.

89. Curt Gentry, *J. Edgar Hoover: The Man and the Secrets* (New York: Norton, 2001).

90. John F. Fox Jr., "In the Enemy's House: Venona and the Maturation of American Counterintelligence," presentation, October 27, 2005, https://www.fbi.gov/history/history-publications-reports/in-the-enemys-house-venona-and-the-maturation-of-american-counterintelligence.

91. FBI, "William Remington," https://vault.fbi.gov/william-remington.

92. Robert L. Benson, "The Venona Story," The Center of Cryptologic History, https://www.nsa.gov/portals/75/documents/about/cryptologic-heritage/historical-figures-publications/publications/coldwar/venona_story.pdf.

93. Liza Mundy, "Secrets of History: The Women Code Breakers Who Unmasked Soviet Spies," *Smithsonian Magazine*, September 2018, https://www.smithsonianmag.com/history/women-code-breakers-unmasked-soviet-spies-180970034/.

94. Robert Louis Benson and Michael Warner, eds., *Venona: Soviet Espionage and the American Response 1939–1957* (Washington, D.C.: National Security Agency, 1996), https://babel.hathitrust.org/cgi/pt?id=mdp.39015038521723&seq=29&q1=weisband.

95. Ronald Kessler, *The Bureau: The Secret History of the FBI* (New York: St. Martin's Press, 2002), https://archive.org/details/bureau00rona.

96. *Supplementary Detailed Staff Reports on Intelligence Activities and the Rights of Americans*, Book III, *Final Report of the Select Committee to Study Governmental Operations* (Washington, D.C.: U.S. Government Printing Office, 1976), https://www.intelligence.senate.gov/sites/default/files/94755_III.pdf.

97. FBI, "The FBI Academy: A Pictorial History," https://www.fbi.gov/history/the-fbi-academy-a-pictorial-history.

9. Infamous Soviet Moles Arrested by the FBI

98. FBI, "Earl Pitts Chair," https://www.fbi.gov/history/artifacts/earl-pitts-chair.

99. WayBack Machine, "FBI Press Release: U.S. Department of Justice Federal Bureau of Investigation," Wednesday, December 18, 1996, https://web.archive.org/web/20031209102034/http://www.loyola.edu/dept/politics/intel/pitts.html.

100. Christopher Burgess, "Spy History: The FBI Special Agent Who Sold His Secrets to the KGB," Clearance Jobs, December 18, 2021, https://news.clearancejobs.com/2021/12/18/spy-history-the-fbi-special-agent-who-sold-his-secrets-to-the-kgb/.

101. Marie Brenner, "The Unquiet American," *Washington Post*, September 21, 1997, https://www.washingtonpost.com/archive/lifestyle/magazine/1997/09/21/the-unquiet-american/dd02e2e5-c645-490c-9583-aa6769072f37/.

102. Faye Fiore, "FBI Admits It Dismissed 1997 Tip about Hanssen," *Los Angeles Times*, May 29, 2001, https://www.latimes.com/archives/la-xpm-2001-may-29-mn-3802-story.html.

103. FBI, "John Anthony Walker Jr. Spy Case," https://www.fbi.gov/history/artifacts/john-anthony-walker-jr-spy-case.

104. Sturdevant, *Cold War Illinois*.

105. David Wise, *Spy: The Inside Story of How the FBI's Robert Hanssen Betrayed America* (New York: Random House, 2002).

106. David Wise, "Thirty Years Later, We Still Don't Truly Know Who Betrayed These Spies. Was There a Fourth Mole in the U.S. Intelligence System That Blew These Secret Agents' Covers?" *Smithsonian Magazine*, November 2015, https://www.smithsonianmag.com/history/still-unexplained-cold-war-fbi-cia-180956969/.

107. FBI, "Hanssen 'Ellis' Drop Site," https://www.fbi.gov/image-repository/hanssen-drop-site.jpeg/.

108. Federation of American Scientists, "An Assessment of the Aldrich H. Ames Espionage Case and Its Implications for U.S. Intelligence Senate Select Committee on Intelligence Part One November 1, 1994," Intelligence Resource Program, https://irp.fas.org/congress/1994_rpt/ssci_ames.htm.

109. Tim Weiner, "Why I Spied: Aldrich Ames," *New York Times Magazine*, July 31, 1994, https://www.nytimes.com/1994/07/31/magazine/why-i-spied-aldrich-ames.html.

110. Adrienne Wilmoth Lerner, "Ames (Aldrich H.) Espionage Case," Encyclopedia.com, https://www.encyclopedia.com/history/united-states-and-canada/us-history/ames-espionage-case.

111. FBI, "Aldrich Ames: Famous Cases and Criminals," https://www.fbi.gov/history/famous-cases/aldrich-ames.

10. General George C. Marshall and the Marshall Plan

112. David L. Roll, *George Marshall: Defender of the Republic* (New York: Dutton Caliber, 2019).
113. Ibid.
114. Sturdevant, *Cold War Wisconsin*, 30–35.
115. National Archives, "Truman Doctrine (1947)," https://www.archives. gov/milestone-documents/truman-doctrine.
116. Visit Loudoun, "George C. Marshall's Dodona Manor," https://www. visitloudoun.org/listing/george-c-marshalls-dodona-manor/13/.

11. Francis Gary Powers and the U-2 Incident

117. Research and recollections of Francis Gary Powers Jr.
118. Hall of Valor Project, "Francis Gary Powers," http://valor. militarytimes.com/recipient.php?recipientid=33580).

12. Notable Cold War Virginians

119. Chesapeake Conservancy, "The Honorable John Warner, Former U.S. Senator of Virginia," https://www.chesapeakeconservancy.org/ champions-of-the-chesapeake/champions-2016/honorable-john- warner-former-u-s-senator-virginia/.
120. Agreement Between the Government of The United States of America and the Government of The Union of Soviet Socialist Republics on the Prevention of Incidents On and Over the High Seas, https://2009-2017.state.gov/t/isn/4791.htm.
121. Carl Hulse, "John Warner, Genteel Senator from Virginia, Dies at 94," *New York Times*, May 26, 2021, https://www.nytimes. com/2021/05/26/us/politics/john-warner-genteel-senator-from- virginia-dies-at-94.html.
122. Thomas Spoehr, "Remembering Reagan's Army Secretary, John O. Marsh Jr.," February 5, 2019, https://www.heritage.org/defense/ commentary/remembering-reagans-army-secretary-john-o-marsh-jr.
123. The Hall of Valor Project, "James Henry Webb," https://valor. militarytimes.com/hero/4226.

124. Naval Heritage and History Command, "James H. Webb, 9 February 1946," https://www.history.navy.mil/content/history/nhhc/browse-by-topic/people/sec-nav/webb/james-webb.html.

125. Alumni Park, "Charles Robb, U.S. Senator," https://www.alumnipark.com/exhibits/featured/charles-robb/.

126. WayBack Machine, "Charles S. Robb, Distinguished Professor of Law & Public Policy 2007," https://web.archive.org/web/20080316044639/http://www.law.gmu.edu/faculty/directory/robb_charles.

127. Encyclopedia Virginia, "Charles S. Robb," https://encyclopediavirginia.org/entries/robb-charles-s-1939/.

13. Doomsday Planning for the Third World War

128. Matt Novak, "The Fed's Cold War Bunker Had $4 Billion Cash for after the Apocalypse," Gizmodo, April 24, 2015, https://gizmodo.com/the-feds-cold-war-bunker-had-4-billion-cash-for-after-1699204253.

129. The White House Communications Agency: A Look into Its Past, Present and Future, "Presidential Emergency Facility Site 3 – 'Cowpuncher' (1965)-revised," https://whcacannonball.blogspot.com/p/presidential-emergency-facility-site-3.html.

130. NPR, "The Secret Bunker Congress Never Used, National Public Radio," *All Things Considered*, March 26, 2011, https://www.npr.org/2011/03/26/134379296/the-secret-bunker-congress-never-used.

131. Site Data on Kate's Mountain Rd., Greenbrier State Forest, Greenbrier County, West Virginia, https://long-lines.net/places-routes/Kates_Mtn/index.html.

132. Interior Department Bomb Shelter Harpers Ferry, WV, https://coldwar-c4i.net/Harpers_Ferry/index.html.

133. Mount Weather High Point Special Facility (SF) Mount Weather Emergency Assistance Center [MWEAC], https://www.globalsecurity.org/wmd/facility/mt_weather.htm.

INDEX

A

Abel, Rudolf 104, 129, 134
Air Force 27, 31, 41, 42, 43, 58, 89,
        135, 136, 140, 141, 145, 149
Allied intervention into Russia 70, 86
Ames, Aldrich 109, 116, 117, 118
Atoms for Peace 73, 74, 78, 79, 80

B

Beirut 49, 97, 149
Boeing Michigan Aeronautical
        Research Center 58, 59
Bolsheviks 70, 71, 100

C

Castro, Fidel 12, 92, 93
Central Intelligence Agency 41,
        42, 55, 59, 83, 88, 89, 91, 92,
        104, 118, 125, 135, 136
Chernobyl 7, 15, 79
China 12, 42, 43, 85, 96, 121, 123,
        136, 151

Churchill, Winston 70, 86, 128
COINTELPRO 89, 105
Containment Policy 124
Cuba 12, 16, 51, 92, 93, 136
Culpeper Switch 152

D

Dodona Manor 121, 127
Donovan, William J. "Wild Bill"
        71, 86, 87

E

Eisenhower, Dwight D. 42, 73, 74,
        78, 79, 88, 89, 129, 136, 154

F

Federal Bureau of Investigation 86,
        99, 102, 105, 113

G

Gagarin, Yuri 33, 34
Giancana, Salvatore 92, 93, 94
Gorbachev, Mikhail 13, 50, 90
Grabeel, Gene 103
Greenbrier Hotel 154

H

Hanssen, Robert 109, 111, 113, 114, 115, 116
Haywood, William Dudley "Big Bill" 69
Hoover, Herbert 69
Hoover, J. Edgar 69, 100, 101, 105, 106, 107

I

International Workers of the World 69
Iran 12, 79, 80, 95, 148

K

Kennan, George 124
Kennedy, John F. 35, 36, 37, 42, 51, 88, 92, 158
Khrushchev, Nikita 22, 27, 29, 94
Khrushchev, Sergei 22, 27, 29
King, Martin Luther, Jr. 106
Korolev, Sergei 27, 30

L

Langley Air Force Base 54, 59

M

Marine Corps 45, 46, 47, 48, 49, 55, 107, 149, 150

Marshall, George C. 121, 123, 124, 126, 127, 128
Marshall Plan 124, 125, 126, 127
moon landing 7

N

NASA 16, 20, 27, 31, 32, 35, 36, 38, 39
National Reconnaissance Office 41, 43
NATO 9, 47, 50, 127
Nike missile 8, 16, 19, 20, 22, 23, 24, 25, 29, 57, 58
Nixon, Richard 85, 106, 147, 148
Norfolk, Virginia 16, 23, 24, 50, 51, 52, 57, 58
NS *Savannah* 73, 74, 76, 77

O

Operation Overflight 130, 138
Operation Rollback 90, 92, 124, 125

P

Pentagon, United States 62, 64, 113, 121
Pitts, Earl Edwin 109, 110, 111
Powers, Francis Gary 16, 41, 88, 105, 129, 130, 133, 134, 135, 140, 141
Powers, Francis Gary, Jr. 61, 130, 133

Q

Quantico 45, 46, 107, 109

R

Radford Ammunition Plant 16, 52
Radio Free Europe 89
Radio Liberty 89
Reagan, Ronald 12, 13, 49, 50, 52,
    95, 106, 143, 148
Red Scare 85, 100
Red Squads 113
Robb, Charles 150

S

Soviet Union 9, 13, 15, 16, 17, 20,
    23, 24, 27, 29, 38, 41, 42, 43,
    49, 50, 57, 58, 65, 69, 72, 73,
    74, 85, 86, 88, 89, 90, 94,
    101, 102, 105, 109, 111, 112,
    114, 115, 116, 118, 123, 124,
    127, 130, 132, 133, 136, 142,
    145, 147, 148, 151
Space Shuttle 7, 40
Space Station 38, 39
Sputnik 12, 27, 29, 33, 41
Stalin, Joseph 9, 67, 70, 89, 114,
    124, 127

T

Truman, Harry 9, 87, 88, 121, 123,
    124, 125, 126

U

U-2 program 42, 135, 145

V

Venona Project 102, 103
Vint Hill Farms Station 60
von Braun, Wernher 20, 30, 32

W

Walker, John, Jr. 109, 112, 116
Warner, John 147
Webb, Jim 149
Wilson, Woodrow 55, 67, 68, 69,
    70, 71, 72, 86

Y

Yeager, Chuck 31, 32

ABOUT THE AUTHORS

FRANCIS GARY POWERS JR. is the founder and chairman emeritus of The Cold War Museum, a 501(c) (3) charity in Vint Hill, Virginia, near Washington, D.C. As chairman of the Presidential Advisory Committee for the Cold War Theme Study, he worked with the National Park Service and leading Cold War experts to identify historic Cold War sites for commemoration, interpretation and preservation. He served as a consultant to Steven Spielberg's Cold War thriller *Bridge of Spies*. Gary is an award-winning author,  lectures internationally and appears regularly on the History, Discovery and A&E channels.

 CHRISTOPHER STURDEVANT is a children's librarian who resides in Milwaukee, Wisconsin. His interest in the Cold War began while growing up during the 1980s. Chris studied history and physics at Carroll University. He is a U.S. Air Force veteran and chairman of the Midwest Chapter of The Cold War Museum in Washington, D.C. In addition, Chris has represented Team USA in master's-level track championships on three continents. His travels have taken him to North Korea, Chernobyl and Afghanistan.